# VERGIL'S METRE

A Practical Guide for Reading
Latin Hexameter Poetry

by
## G.B. Nussbaum
University of Keele

Published by Bristol Classical Press
General Editor: John H. Betts

First published in 1986 by
Bristol Classical Press
an imprint of
Gerald Duckworth & Co. Ltd
61 Frith Street
London W1D 3JL
e-mail: inquiries@duckworth-publishers.co.uk
Website: www.ducknet.co.uk

Reprinted 1990, 2001

A catalogue record for this book is available
from the British Library

ISBN 0-86292-173-2

# CONTENTS

TO THE READER


Like its companion *Homer's Metre*, this booklet is presented
as a practical guide on 'do-it-yourself' lines. This is not
really to suggest that many people are likely to master the
hexameter without the help of a teacher. But it should encourage motivated students to do as much as they comfortably
can on their own.

To this end, please feel free to use the booklet in whatever
way you find helpful. If you cannot cover it all, be selective,
perhaps coming back to some sections later. Above all, do not
feel that you must labour over non-essentials that you find
obscure or overloading: these too may fall into place later
on. This applies particularly to some of the refinements,
a few of them quite important, which have been kept to the
notes at the back. As for the step-by-step learning method
used in Parts IV-VII, that too is a resource to be taken
advantage of, if it proves useful - and not some kind of
obligatory ritual!

Theory does figure in this presentation. Where it becomes
more extended or technical, it is reserved to the appendices
and notes at the back, to which you can turn as interest
prompts. Some theory is necessary to give a basic understanding and to inform practice. But theory is important
for another reason as well. For if the primary aim of this
booklet is to lead newcomers to an authentic reading of the
hexameter, its secondary aim is to provide the basis for
much literary appreciation of the poetry, for understanding
many a point of artistry and of meaning that is brought out
by editors and writers on Vergil - and which you may also
discover for yourself.

# PREFACE

Like its companion, *Homer's Metre*, this booklet is intended
as a practical guide.  Theory figures in it insofar as it
is needed to inform practice; where it is developed and becomes more technical it is kept to the notes or appendices.
Some theoretically important distinctions are ignored, as
for example when syllables are called 'long' and 'short',
even though these terms should be reserved for vowels,
while syllables should be called 'heavy' and 'light'.
Teaching experience has convinced me that the attempt to
observe this distinction proves to be an extra hurdle
rather than a useful clarification (see note 11).

In some ways, learning to read Latin hexameters should be
easier than Greek.  The script and punctuation are familiar,
and in matters of pronunciation and of the identification
of syllables the balance may also be in favour of Latin.
Yet the mastering of the hexameter is a larger enterprise
in Latin than it is in Greek.  One reason for this is the
troublesome phenomenon of vowel-junction (elision) in
Latin, which Greek avoids by the use of the apostrophe for
final short vowels and of 'epic hastening' (epic correption)
for long ones.  This extra topic claims an important place
in learning the rhythm (Part IV), and a whole appendix to
itself.

But perhaps the most important difference is the interplay of
verse-beat and word-accent (ictus and accent); which operates
in Latin as it does in English, but not in Greek.  This adds
a whole dimension to Latin hexameter poetry – and an extra
section to this booklet (Part VII).  My treatment is based
on the hypothesis that Vergil and his contemporaries read in
a way which did not drum out the metre and distort the word-
accents, yet was audibly different from the reading of prose.
In practice, I believe that newcomers must first learn the
rhythm of the metre (as the Romans did at school) and master
the phrasing of the verse, otherwise they do in fact simply
treat the text as prose.  The 'counterpoint' of ictus and
accent is then left as the crowning achievement in acquiring
this demanding and rewarding art: it is the key, not only to
authentic reading, but also to the discerning of a wealth
of poetic artistry.  Since my hypothesis on ictus-accent interplay may be controversial, I note here that in the 2nd edition
of his *Vox Latina* (1978) Prof. W.S. Allen has modified his
earlier view, which had favoured a purely metrical reading
with suppression of the word-accent.  This is still the view
of the *text* of the 2nd edition, at pp.92-4, which is simply
a reprint of the 1st edition of 1965.  But in the new material
on p.126, based on the findings of his own intervening *Accent
and Rhythm* (1973), we read: 'The evidence seems to suggest
that in fact it was normal to recite Latin verse with the
natural word (and/or sentence) stresses, rather than with the

regular but artificial verse ictus - though this precluded
any clear dynamic pattern from emerging in the first four
feet of the hexameter,' yet, I would add, still allowed the
ictus to be realised aurally in counterpoint with the dominant word-accent.

Mention of Prof. Allen naturally leads on to the acknowledge-
ment of my debts, in which his name, together with those of
L.P. Wilkinson (especially in his *Golden Latin Artistry*)
and D.S. Raven (in *Latin Metre*), must stand out from the
cumulative and anonymous background of many years' study.
Of course I retain sole responsibility for my views and
methods, which are set forth more fully in my 'On the
Authentic Reading of Hexameter Poetry', *Aufstieg und
Niedergang der Römischen Welt* II 35, forthcoming.

One other debt I must acknowledge - to generations of students
in Latin or Roman Studies at Keele University (as also in Greek
Studies for my *Homer's Metre*), the unwitting guinea-pigs
who have 'benefited' from my search for a way of learning to
read Vergil as authentically as possible. Those of us who
teach the hexameter mostly learned to read it some time ago,
within a theoretical framework that now looks less than wholly
satisfactory or comprehensive, but with more time and more
Latin at our disposal than most of our students have today.
Perhaps we were hardly aware of the minor triumph that it
was, for us too, to become fluent readers of the hexameter -
and we were those destined to become specialists! Nor does
the expert always find it easy to enter imaginatively into
the learning processes of newcomers, and to maintain an
approach that works from inside their situation rather than
his or her own. This booklet is an attempt to lead beginners
gently, and from within their own comprehension at each step,
as far as they want to go towards a full, confident and (within our limitations) authentic reading of Vergil.

G. Nussbaum
Keele
October, 1986

# INTRODUCTION

Vergil's metre is called the hexameter - a Greek name for
a Greek metre. It is the metre of the earliest known poetry
of Europe, the *Iliad* and the *Odyssey* of Homer. Because it
is so early in its origins, we might have expected this metre
to be quite simple. Far from it. The hexameter is a mar-
vellous creation in its own right. Impressive in its sheer
length (just under 16 syllables on average in Greek, nearer
14 in Latin, yet the line maintains a strong sense of organic
unity. Its secret lies in the play of variation on a fixed
ground-plan of six stresses and a mid-line division. As line
follows line, we are presented with ever-shifting versions
of the same basic identity.[1] Moreover, the metre interacts
with the natural phrasing of the sense as an integral part
of reading.

Such a metre cannot be picked up casually; it has to be carefully learned. The aim of this booklet is to offer, first, an
understanding of the hexameter, and then a practical method
for learning to read the poetry fluently, with a clear and
ready sense both of rhythm and of the interplay between the
metre and the meaning through the phrasing of the text. And
here let us be clear about one thing: to read Vergil authentically is to read him aloud. This is not a question of the
original 'oral', or unwritten, character of Greek hexameter
verse. It is simply that ancient poets, Roman as well as
Greek, never composed primarily for the page and for the eye,
though they did use writing as an *aide-memoire* - perhaps
even Homer, whoever he was or whoever they were. Poetry
belonged first and foremost to the voice and to the ear, and
to read it was to read it, and to hear it read, aloud.

500 years after Homer, and 150 years before Vergil, the
Greek hexameter was naturalised into Latin. The genius of
the Latin language is different from that of Greek. For
one thing, Latin has fewer short and more long syllables
than Greek, making for a slower, heavier movement, less
fluid and lively, more solid and intense.[2] Above all, the
rules of the dominant Latin stress accent are different
from those governing the subsidiary Greek stress accent,
on which the rhythm of the Greek hexameter is based.[3] In
Greek, the beat of the metre coincides with the natural stress
of the words. In Latin, the two sometimes coincide on the
same syllable, sometimes fall on different syllables. This
gives the Latin hexameter a kind of counterpoint between
verse-beat and word-accent which is missing from the Greek
- to whose light and rapid movement it would actually be quite
unsuited; whereas without this counterpoint Latin hexameter
poetry would be ponderous and dull (see n20 , and Appendix V).

Three things are assumed at the outset:

(i)   the ability to read Latin with reasonable fluency;
(ii)  the ability to divide words into syllables.  The theory
      of how vowels and consonants are grouped together to
      form syllables is actually quite subtle, but for our
      purpose all we need is a reasonable ready sense of
      syllable following syllable, as an automatic part of
      the process of reading - and the ability to check it
      out if need be;
(iii) an understanding of how words are combined to form the
      units of meaning (sentences, clauses etc.); and, in
      poetry, also the unit by which the metre is commonly
      identified, namely, the verse or line.

The key to the easy use of this booklet is the list of special
markings and the specimen text, given in two versions:  version
A for use throughout Parts II-V, and version B for use with
parts VI and VII and Appendix III. (A photocopy of these pages
will enable the reader to work through the booklet, without
the need for continual back-reference.)


*Reading Hexameters and Traditional Scansion (see also Appendix V).*

The method here offered rests on the assumption that the Latin
hexameter, derived from the Greek, has a clear rhythm, formed
by a sequence of six stressed syllables with a regular mid-line
division.  It begins by offering, in Parts II and III,
a tangible experience and a basic understanding of this pattern.
In traditional scansion, we learn to write out each line broken
up into its six 'feet' yet without any explicit rhythm.  Here,
instead, the marking of six syllables in the printed text
with a ' placed above the vowel clearly shows the rhythm of each
line without losing the feet.  A seventh marking, a ¦ placed
between two words, shows the two-part structure - and all
without dismembering the line in the process.  A method for
doing this is given in Part IV.  Hopefully, it is simpler and
more useful in practice, perhaps also more satisfactory in
theory.  Moreover, it goes on quite naturally to cover the
interplay of the metre and the meaning through the phrasing
of the text (Part V).

On the basis of a clear sense of the rhythm and structure of
the line (Part VI), we are then able to go on again quite
naturally in Part VII to cover the counterpoint between the
verse-beat or ictus (marked ') and the normal word-accent
(marked with an extended French acute above the vowel: ╱ , with
a ✓ (a tick to show their coincidence).  Here we have a major
extra dimension, absent from Greek, in the mastery of the
hexameter.  Yet without it we must either drum out the metre,
thereby violating the natural stress of many words; or if we
read the verse just like prose, we weaken the metre and,
either way, we lose the counterpoint. [4]

In the end, all this has to happen just from the plain text, and a kind of weaning process to dispense with the markings is included in Parts VI and VII. All the way through, the aim is to encourage real live reading of Vergil, as authentic as possible - hence also the Pronunciation Checklist. The hexameter, especially the mature Latin hexameter of Vergil, does not yield up its treasures easily - but they are rich indeed. The various aspects covered in this booklet do not merely provide the ground-rules of Vergil's poetry; they are at the same time the key to a great part of his complex, many-levelled artistic creativity. Even Tennyson did not fully do justice to the incomparable blend of power and subtlety in Vergil's hexameter when he called Vergil 'Wielder of the stateliest measure ever moulded by the lips of man'.

## PART IA: SPECIAL MARKINGS AND SPECIMEN TEXT

*(N.B. By making a copy of these markings and the specimen
texts, the reader will be able to refer to them easily
throughout.)*

— *long:* placed over the vowel of a long syllable, e.g.
  *mōntīs* (see note 11). Diphthongs are long, and are so
  marked on their second vowel, e.g. *caprāe.*

˘ *short:* placed over the vowel of a short syllable, e.g.
  *uērtĭcĕ.*

– *vowel-junction:* the hyphen is used to join two words of
  which the first ends in a vowel or *m* and the second begins
  with a vowel or *h*, e.g. *atque-inuia, postquam-altos, iamque-
  hos* (see note 13). *Note:* the hyphen has no other use in
  Latin poetry.

' *ictus:* placed over the vowel of the syllable bearing the
  verse-beat, e.g. *pòstquam-altòs.*

/ *accent:* placed over the vowel of a syllable bearing the
  natural word-accent, e.g. *férae sáxi.*

∨ *ictus and accent:* placed over the vowel of a syllable on
  which ictus and accent coincide, e.g. *ĕcce fĕraè sáxi
  deiĕctae uĕrtice cáprae.*

⋮ *caesura:* placed between two words at the mid-line division,
  e.g. *ecce ferae saxi ⋮ deiectae uertice caprae.*

/ *minor pause,* and

// *major pause:* used to mark the phrasing of the metre and the
  sense both at the line-end and within the line, e.g. *ecce
  ferae saxi ⋮ deiectae uertice caprae /* and *decurrere
  iugis; ⋮ //.*

4

*Specimen Text, version A:*   *Aeneid* 4.151-72.

## Section 1

1.
```
    1      4        2   3      5       6    7        8
POSTQUAM-ALTOS VENTUM-IN  MONTIS  ATQUE-INVIA   LUSTRA,
After   · high  coming into mountains and    pathless haunts
```

2.
```
   1     2     6        4        5          3
ECCE  FERAE SAXI    DEIECTAE  VERTICE     CAPRAE
look! wild  of-a-rock thrown-down from-the-top goats
```

3.
```
     7         8       2        1   3      6
DECURRERE   IUGIS;   ALIA     DE PARTE PATENTIS
have-run-down the-slopes the-other on side   open
```

4.
```
      5       8        7    9    13      4
TRANSMITTUNT CURSU  CAMPOS ATQUE-AGMINA CERVI
move-across  at-a-run plains and    columns deer
```

5.
```
     12    10           11         16  14
PULVERULENTA FUGA    GLOMERANT   MONTISQUE
dusty       in-flight mass-together the-mountains-and
```
```
     15
RELIQUUNT.
leave-behind
```

## Section 2

6.
```
  1,    2      3,    5,       4    6      8
AT   PUER  ASCANIUS : MEDIIS     IN VALLIBUS ACRI
But the-boy Ascanius  the-middle-of in the valley on-his-keen
```

7.
```
   7       9     11 10  13    14      15    12     16
GAUDET  EQUO IAMQUE- HOS : CURSU,  IAM PRAETERIT ILLOS,
rejoices horse now-and these at-speed now overtakes those
```

8.
    ,3  ,1   5,           9    ,7   ,8
SPUMANTEMQUE  DARI :      PECORA- INTER INERTIA

a-foaming-and to-be-granted animals among the-feeble (in

     ,6
    VOTIS

answer) to-his-prayers


9.
    ,2         4    10  11,     13      ,14
OPTAT        APRUM,-AUT FULVUM : DESCENDERE   MONTE

he-longs-for boar    or  a-tawny  to-come-down from-the-

       12
    LEONEM.

mountain lion


Section 3

10.
    ,1  ,5 ,       4,       ,6    2
INTEREA  MAGNO :    MISCERI        MURMURE  CAELUM /

Meantime with-a-great to-grow-confused rumbling the-sky


11.
    ,3    ,7   ,     9,     10     8
INCIPIT, / INSEQUITUR : COMMIXTA    GRANDINE NIMBUS; //

begins    there-follows with-mixed-in hail   a-storm-cloud


12.
1    2,       3,   4   5   6,     ,7
ET  TYRII    COMITES : PASSIM- ET TROIANA   IUVENTUS /

Both the-Tyrian companions every-way and the-Trojan youth


13.
    ,9  ,8    10     11,    13 16   ,17
DARDANIUSQUE   NEPOS : VENERIS DIVERSA PER   AGROS /

the-Dardan-and grandson of-Venus distant across the-countryside


14.
  ,14   15,    12,     2,   3   ,4   ,1
TECTA    METU   PETIERE; //  RUUNT : DE  MONTIBUS AMNES //

shelters in-fear have-sought  rush down-from the mountains rivers

Section 4

```
        7         1        4       2       3          6
15.  SPELUNCAM DIDO : DUX    ET    TROIANUS    EANDEM   /

     cave       Dido    leader and the-Trojan to-the-same
```

```
        5  ·              2    1      3        4        6
16.  DEVENIUNT. //   PRIMA ET   TELLUS : ET   PRONUBA

     find-their-way.Primaeval both Earth and (goddess of marriage)
                                                    .5
                                              IUNO /
                                              Juno
```

```
        7       8            10       9     11           13        12
17.  DANT SIGNUM; //  FULSERE : IGNES / ET          CONSCIUS AETHER /

     give the-signal flashed    fires   and(was) witness    Aether
```

```
        14            18    15               17          19
18.  CONUBIIS /    SUMMOQUE :            ULULARUNT VERTICE

     to-the-wedding on-the-topmost-and wailed      peak
                                                    16
                                              NYMPHAE. //

                                              Nymphs
```

```
        1     2     3       6       8      7      9
19.  ILLE DIES PRIMUS : LETI    PRIMUSQUE MALORUM /

     That day  first   of death first-and of-ills
```

```
        5         4        2       1     4
20.  CAUSA     FUIT; //  NEQUE  ENIM : SPECIE

     the-cause became    neither for   by-appearances
                              6 5                3
                              FAMAVE           MOVETUR, //

                         by-reputation-or is-she-moved
```

```
        7   8         11      9      10          12
21.  NEC IAM    FURTIVUM : DIDO MEDITATUR    AMOREM: //

     nor any-longer a-secret Dido is brooding-on love:
```

```
        13          14              15          17
22.  CONIUGIUM VOCAT, /          HOC :    PRAETEXIT

     marriage  she-calls (it)  with-this she-veils
                                    16      18
                                NOMINE CULPAM. //

                                name    (her)-guilt.
```

*Specimen Text, version B: Aeneid 4.151-72.*

```
        / 1      / 4_    / 2  _3    / 5     _6 / 7_     /8_
1.  POSTQUAM-ALTOS VENTUM-IN  MONTIS   ATQUE-INVIĂ  LUSTRA,

    After     high   coming into mountains and   pathless haunts
```

```
     / 1     /2_    /6_          /4_      / 5        / 3_
2.  ECCĔ FĔRAE SAXI      DEIECTAE   VERTĬCĔ      CAPRAE

    look wild  of-a-rock thrown-down from-the-top goats
```

```
     / _7 /       /8         /2_      1_ /3     /6_
3.  DECURRERĔ    IUGIS;    ALIĂ    DE PARTĔ PĂTENTIS

    have-run-down the-slopes; the-other on side   open
```

```
        5/     _ /8_      /7    _9  / 13   / 4_
4.  TRANSMITTUNT CURSU  CAMPOS ATQUE-AGMĬNĂ CERVI

    move-across  at-a-run plains and   columns deer
```

```
     /  12 /    /0_         /11        16 / 14_
5.  PULVĔRULĔNTĂ FUGA    GLOMĔRANT   MONTISQUĔ

    dusty        in-flight mass-together the-mountains-and
                                              /15_
                                        RĔLINQUUNT.

                                        leave-behind
```

Section 2

6.
|   | 1 | 2 | 3 | 5 | 4 | 6 | 8 |
AT PUER ASCANIUS : MEDIIS IN VALLIBUS ACRI

But the-boy Ascanius    the-middle-of in the-valley on-his-keen

7.
|   | 7 | 9 | 11 | 10 | 13 | 14 | 15 | 12 | 16 |
GAUDET EQUO IAMQUE- HOS : CURSU, IAM PRAETERIT ILLOS,

rejoices horse now-and these at speed now overtakes those

8.
|   | 3 | 1 | 5 | 9 | 7 | 8 |
SPUMANTEMQUE DARI : PECORA- INTER INERTIA

a-foaming-and to-be-granted animals among the-feeble(in answer)

                                    6
                                  VOTIS

                                  to-his-prayers

9.
|   | 2 | 4 | 10 | 11 | 13 |
OPTAT APRUM,- AUT FULVUM : DESCENDERE

he-long-for boar   . or  a-tawny  to-come-down

                        14                    12
                      MONTE                  LEONEM

                    from-the-mountain lion

Section 3

10.
|   | 1 | 5 | 4 | 6 | 2 |
INTEREA MAGNO : MISCERI MURMURE CAELUM /

Meantime with-a-great to-grow-confused rumbling the-sky

11.
|   | 3 | 7 | 9 | 10 | 8 |
INCIPIT/ INSEQUITUR ! COMMIXTA GRANDINE NIMBUS . //

begins   there-follows with-mixed-in hail   a-storm-cloud

12.  ET  TYRII     COMITES : PASSIM- ET TROIANA
        ¹    ²        ³     ⁴     5    6

Both the-Tyrian companions every-way and the-Trojan

                                ⁷
                           IUVENTUS /

                           youth

13.  DARDANIUSQUE NEPOS : VENERIS DIVERSA PER
          ⁹     ⁸     ¹⁰     ¹¹    ¹³ 16

the-Dardan-and grandson of-Venus distant across

                            ¹⁷
                       AGROS /

                       the-countryside

14.  TECTA   METU  PETIERE; // RUUNT : DE
        ¹⁴    ¹⁵    ¹²     ¹⁹   20

shelters in-fear have-sought rush   down-from

                   ²¹          ¹⁸
               MONTIBUS    AMNES. //

              the-mountains rivers

Section 4

15.  SPELUNCAM DIDO : DUX  ET  TROIANUS  EANDEM /
        7      1    4    2    3       6

    cave      Dido    leader and the-Trojan to-the-same

16.  DEVENIUNT. // PRIMA ET  TELLUS : ET PRONUBA
      5          2   1     3     4   6

find-their-way Primaeval both Earth and (goddess)of-marriage

                                5
                          IUNO/

                          Juno

17.  DANT SIGNUM; // FULSERE : IGNES / ET     CONSCIUS AETHER /
      7   8      10     9   11         13   12

    give the-signal flashed  fires  and(was) witness Aether

```
            14              18    15               17          19
18.  CONUBIIS /      SOMMOQUE :           ULULARUNT VERTICE
     to-the-wedding on-the-topmost-and wailed      peak
                                           16
                                         NYMPHAE. //

                                         Nymphs


       1     2     3       6        8      7      9
19.  ILLE DIES PRIMUS : LETI     PRIMUSQUE MALORUM /
     That day first    of-death first-and of-ills


       5       4       2      1      4
20.  CAUSA   FUIT; // NEQUE  ENIM : SPECIE
     the-cause became  Neither for   by-appearances
                              6 5             3
                            FAMAVE        MOVETUR, //

                            by-reputation-or is-she-moved


      7   8           11     9     10           12
21.  NEC IAM      FURTIVUM : DIDO MEDITATUR   AMOREM: //
     nor any-longer a-secret  Dido is-brooding-on love:


       13      14          15        17      16
22.  CONIUGIUM VOCAT, /   HOC :   PRAETEXIT NOMINE
     marriage she-calls(it) with-this she-veils name
                                    18
                                  CULPAM. //

                                  (her)-guilt.
```

# PART IB: PRONUNCIATION CHECKLIST

The standard guide to the pronunciation of Classical Latin is *Vox Latina* by W.S. Allen (2nd edn.: CUP, 1978). In this checklist we shall be content at times with approximate equivalents in English or, occasionally, in another modern language.

*Alphabetic List*

ă     short *a*: like standard English *u* in 'cup'.
ā     long *a*: like English *a* in 'master'.
ae    diphthong: like English *i* in 'bite'.
au    diphthong: like English *ou* in 'house'; more like German *au* in 'Haus'.
b     like English *b*; before *s* and *t* = *p*.
c     commonly pronounced like English *k*; before a vowel, strictly like the French hard *c*.
ch    like the English strong *c* or *k* before a vowel.
d     like English *d*.
ě     short *e*: like English *e* in 'get'.
ē     long *e*: like *ee* in 'Beethoven'.
ei    diphthong: like the *ey* in 'grey'.
eu    diphthong: = ě+ǔ in quick succession; no real English equivalent, commonly pronounced like 'you'.
f     like English *f*.
g     like English hard *g* in 'get'.
gn    = ngn, e.g. magnus = mangnus.
h     like English *h*; does not count as a consonant in deciding syllable quantity.
ĭ     short *i*: like English *i* in 'bin'.
ī     long *i*: like English *ee* in 'been'.
i     consonant: like English *y* in 'yet'; formerly written as *j* (cf. German 'ja'); occurs where *i* is followed by a vowel *within* the same syllable, e.g. as *y* in *iam*, but as *i* in *fiam* = *fi+am*.
k     like English *k*.
l     like English *l*.
m     like English *m*; at the end of a word *m* is not a consonant, but nasalises the preceding vowel in the combinations -*am*, -*em*, -*im*, -*om* and -*um*.
n     like English *n*; before *c*, *g* and *qu*, *n* = *ng* (as in English 'ankle').
ŏ     short *o*: like English *o* in 'pot'.
ō     long *o*: like Northern English *oa* in 'boat'; more like German *oo* in 'Boot'.
oe    diphthong: like English *oy* in 'boy'.
p     commonly pronounced like English *p*; before a vowel, strictly like the French *p*.
ph    like the English strong *p* before a vowel.
qu    commonly pronounced like English *qu* = *kw*; strictly a single consonant = *k* pronounced with rounded lips.

```
r*   like Italian rolled r; never silent.
s*   like English hard or hissed s.
t    commonly pronounced like English t; before a vowel,
     strictly like French t.
th   like English strong t before a vowel.
ŭ    short u: like English u in 'put'.
ū    long u: like English u in 'Susan'; never like English
     u = yu as in 'use'.
u    consonant: like English w in 'well'; formerly written
     v, and mispronounced as English v; occurs where u is
     followed by a vowel within the same syllable, e.g. as
     w in uis, but as u in suis = su-is.
x    double consonant = ks: like English x in 'axe'; never
     like English x in 'example'.
y    = Greek u, like French u or German ü.
z    like English z.
*    the two consonants r and s are responsible between them
     for a large proportion of mispronunciations by English
     speakers of Latin.  Remember always to sound the r in
     the combinations -ar, -er, -ir, -or and -ur; and to keep
     the s hard in the common ending -es.
```

## Double Consonants and Vowels

In Latin, a doubled consonant *sounds* doubled, or long:
there is a clear difference between *fere* 'almost' and *ferre*
'to carry'.

*ii* and *uu* are common, where the two vowels belong to separate
syllables, e.g. *filii = fi-li-i*, *tuus = tu-us*. The dis-
continuation of the use of *v* for consonantal *u* has undoubtedly
made Latin harder to read, in such words as *seruus, uua*;
occasionally it leads to a spelling like *uoluit*, which may
be either *uo-lu-it* 'he wished', or *uol-uit* 'he rolls'.

## Alternative Spellings

Latin texts can vary a good deal in their spelling, but
apart from the use of *v* for consonantal *u* in older texts,
there is only one variation that need concern us here.  The
accusative plural ending of 3rd declension nouns sometimes
appears as *-es* (remember the hard *s*), and sometimes as *-īs*.
The latter form is nowadays preferred in all those cases
where the genitive plural ends in *-ium* rather than in just
*-um*, which includes nouns in *-is* like *nauis*, and monosyllables
like *urbs*, giving accusative plural *nauīs* and *urbīs* rather
than *naues* and *urbes*.  The same also applies to all 3rd
declension adjectives in *-is* and *-ns*, e.g. *difficilis* and
*amans* give accusative plural *difficilīs* and *amantīs* rather
than *difficiles* and *amantes*, and even *tres* has *trīs* as its
accusative.

There are two points to note here:

1.  Where the accusative plural in the 3rd declension is
    printed as *-is*, remember that this is the long *-īs*,
    and not the short *-ĭs* of the genitive singular or
    of many nominative singulars (the long *-is* also, of
    course, forms the dative and ablative plural of the
    1st and 2nd declensions).

2.  In fact it seems that Vergil may have used both
    endings, *-es* and *-is*, being guided in each case by
    his ear.

*Vowel-Junction ('Elision')*

Where one word ends with a vowel (or *m*), and the next word
begins with a vowel (or *h*), we have a 'vowel-junction'.
This phenomenon is, at least to us, a troublesome compli-
cation of Latin verse. The metre requires the 'knocking-
out' or elision of the first vowel in all such cases. The
traditional pronunciation simply does the same, and this is
certainly the easiest option at first. The subject is taken
up in Part VII, and discussed more fully in Appendix III.

# PART IC: RULES OF WORD-ACCENT


The basic rule governing the Latin accent is as follows:
stress the penultimate syllable of the word (i.e. the last
but one) if it is long (or 'heavy'); if the penultimate is
short (or 'light'), stress the ante-penultimate, i.e. the
last but two, whether this is long or short.

In practice, it may be useful to distinguish as follows:

Three syllable words ('trisyllables') are stressed on their
second syllable if this is long; if the second is short,
the stress falls on the first, whether this is long or short;
e.g.
  deiéctae and paténtis; but ínuĭa, uértĭce and álĭa.

Two-syllable words ('disyllables') are stressed on their
first syllable, whether it is long or short; e.g.
  écce, férae, iúgis and párte

*Note:* In words consisting of two *short* syllables (Pyrrhics),
the accent is optional (see under monosyllables below);
e.g. nĕquĕ, or néquĕ for emphasis (which is it in 20 of the
specimen text?); uŏcăt, as being an important word (22 of
the specimen text), but could also be uŏcát.

Polysyllables (words of four or more syllables) *may* have two
accents, as follows:  their primary accent is the same as
that of trisyllables; their secondary accent is found by
treating the syllables preceding the primary accent as if
they formed a word with its own accent, provided that word
has more than just one long or two short syllables e.g.

  décūrrére, but descéndĕre, petiére, deuénĭunt;
  púluĕrúlénta, but uĭŏléntĭa.

(some envisage a secondary accent in *every* polysyllable, at
least as an option, e.g. déscéndere or pétiére).

Monosyllables (words of one syllable) are best treated as
having an optional accent (cf. the note on Pyrrhics above.)
No doubt some words will normally be unaccented, in particular
prepositions like *ab*, *in* etc. (see note 15), and the word
*et*; while a noun like *urbs* would perhaps always be stressed.
In practice the reader must decide each case on its merits,
according to the importance and emphasis he wants to give
to that word in that context.


*Word-accent and Vowel-junction*

Since the accent is found by counting syllables from the end

of a word, what happens to the accent when a word loses its
final vowel and so becomes one syllable shorter?  It is
normally assumed that this makes no difference to the accent,
but this assumption could be wrong: the question is discussed more fully in the concluding section of Appendix III.
In practice it will be best at first to accent these words
as if they were still whole, with one exception: when the
ending -*que* is elided before a following vowel, we are
left with the main word intact, and accent it accordingly,
e.g. *súmmo* becomes *summóque,* but before a vowel it reverts
to *súmmogu-ulularunt* (specimen text 18).

## PART II: FEELING THE RHYTHM

The specimen text (version A) has been specially marked
so that the reader can pick out the rhythm even before
understanding the sequence of the metre.  There are four
things to note:

1.  *The Beat (ictus)*

Six syllables in each line are marked with the symbol ' to show
they are *stressed*.  So in line 6 the syllables *at, as, us,
is, ual* and *ac* should stand out clearly from the rest,
and the total effect should be as in *tóm-ti-ti tóm-ti-ti
tóm-ti-ti tóm-tom tóm-ti-ti tóm-tom*.  As part III will
show, the sequence of the *tóm-ti-ti* and *tóm-tom* varies,
but there are always the six stresses.  Try the next line,
which gives *tóm-ti-ti tóm-tom tóm-tom tóm-tom tóm-ti-ti
tóm-tom*.  Note that *iamque-hos* is a 'vowel-junction' (since
*h* is not counted as a consonant), and the two syllables *que*
and *hos* run together and count as one:  more of this in
Part IV.  A feeling for the beat should emerge if a similar analysis of lines 8-14 is attempted.


2.  *The Cadence*

The normal hexamter line ends with a highly characteristic
'falling' rhythm, or cadence: *tom-ti-ti tóm-tom*.  So in
line 6 we have *uállibus ácri*; in line 7 *praéterit íllos*;
line 8 *inértia uótis*.  If you try lines 6-14 a feeling for
the recurring rhythm of the ending should emerge.


3.  *The Whole Line*

At this stage, the aim is to feel the rhythm of the hexameter
line as a self-contained unit.  In fact, of course, the sense
will often run on from one line to the next (as in lines 10-
22 of the marked text wherever a line ends with a single /
marking a minor or suspensive pause: see Part V).  But for
the present it will be best to read each line through to the
end, and there make a clear break, though even at this stage
*without dropping the voice* except at a major pause, marked
with the double //.


4.  *The Mid-line Division or Caesura (see note 9)*

Each line also falls into two distinct parts which are
nearly but not exactly equal.  The point at which this
happens is called the 'caesura', and is marked by the symbol :
between two words.  It normally falls immediately after the

17

third stress, sometimes after the fourth. The sense runs
on at this point even more often than at the line-end, and
it is even more important not to drop the voice here except
for a major pause, marked //, which is not common at this
point. Nevertheless, at this stage each line should be
read with some perceptible break at the caesura, so as to
get the feeling of the line as a *two-part* rhythm, rising in
the first half and falling in the second. So for instance
the rhythm of line 6 is: *tóm-ti-ti tóm-ti-ti tóm ∶ -ti-ti
tóm-tom tóm-ti-ti tóm-tom*; that of line 14 is *tóm-ti-ti
tóm-ti-ti tóm-ti-ti tóm ∶ -tom tóm-ti-ti tóm-tom*.

Repeated reading of lines 6-14, ignoring the / and //
markings in lines 10-14 for the moment, should eventually
give a feeling for the total rhythm; i.e. for the six beats,
divided after the third (or, in line 14, after the fourth),
and ending with the cadence.

In reading, the pace will of course vary. But the dominant
pace in Vergil will be rather measured and deliberate, *andante*
rather than *allegro*.

Printed texts of Vergil do not mark the metre; it has to be
worked out by the reader. A practical method for doing this
is offered in Part IV. First, some understanding of what
is happening may be useful, if not indispensable: this is
offered in Part III. But before embarking, first on the
theory and then on the practice, the reader should be able
to feel the rhythm for himself.

## PART III: UNDERSTANDING THE METRE


Beginning with Homer's *Iliad* and *Odyssey*, all Greek
and Latin epic poems use the metre known as the 'dactylic
hexameter' (hexameter for short).


### Dactyls

The Greek word *daktulos* means 'finger'. A finger, from
root to tip along its back, has three parts, of which the
first is roughly equal in length to the other two put together. The dactyl is a sequence of syllables of just this
pattern, that is: long-short-short, marked -ᴗᴗ, where long
counts as equal to twice short. These terms will need more
explanation. For the moment, think of the dactyl simply as
a rhythmic sequence of one stressed syllable followed by
two unstressed ones, giving the rhythm: *tóm-ti-ti*, as in
'ém-pe-ror'.


### Spondees

The two short syllables of the dactyl can be replaced by a
second long one, giving the sequence: long-long, marked
--. This sequence is called the spondee. The stress remains on the first syllable, giving the rhythm: *tóm-tom*,
as in 'ém-pire'.


### The Hexameter

When six (Greek, *hex*) of these two kinds of 'measure'
(Greek, *metron*) are strung together, we have the verse or
line called the hexameter (*hexametron*). In principle, it
is a succession of six dactyls, any of which may be replaced by a spondee.[5]


### Syllable Quantity: Longs and Shorts

The pattern of the hexameter, as of all Classical Greek and
Latin metres, rests on the difference in quantity between
long and short syllables.[6] It is believed that the origins
of Classical poetry were closely bound up with music; and
for those familiar with musical terms, it may be helpful
to think of the syllables as notes having the value (in
two-four time) of a crotchet for a long syllable and a
quaver for a short one. These notes are then grouped into
one of two kinds of bar, both with the same beat, namely:
either crotchet-quaver-quaver = dactyl; or crotchet-crotchet
= spondee.

## Feet

The traditional name for these bars, or groups of syllables,
is 'feet', which may reflect an original link of poetry
with dance as well as music. So the hexameter is said to
have six feet, each of them being either a dactyl or a
spondee, which can then be numbered according to its place
in the line, and called first foot, second foot, etc.

## Verse-beat and Rhythm

But the term 'foot' may also originate from the action of
tapping out the beat rather then from any link with dancing.
Granted that Greek and Latin metres are based on quantity,
that is, on patterns of long and short syllables, they must
also have a rhythm based on verse-beat comparable to a
musical rhythm based on a musical beat. In the hexameter
this beat falls on the first syllable of each of the six
feet. The resulting six-beat sequence gives the hexameter
its rhythm.

## The Cadence

Since dactyls and spondees are wholly interchangeable in the
first four feet, there are many variations in the pattern of
the hexameter line. But the end of the line has a fixed
rhythm, namely: dactyl in the fifth foot and spondee in the
sixth = tŏm-tĭ-tĭ tŏm-tōm, i.e. long-short-short long-long,
as in 'eá-si-ly flów-ing'. This fixed ending gives the
hexameter a powerfully characteristic 'falling' rhythm or
cadence.[8]

## The Caesura[9]

The full name of this mid-line division is the 'central
caesura', and every normal line must have one. It falls
at a word-junction (that is, *between* two words) normally
just after the 3rd beat; if there is no word-junction at
that point, then the caesura falls after the fourth beat
instead. Its effect, as we saw in Part II, is to divide
the line into two almost equal sections, and so to give it
a characteristic two-part flow, first rising and then
falling.

At this point it may benefit the reader to go back to lines
6-14 of the specimen text, and read them over again. Still
the first priority is to *feel* the beat. But it may now be
possible to sense the dactyls and spondees, and, in particular, the rhythm of the cadence; and to enjoy the way in which
the caesura punctuates the succession of six dactyls and
spondees, shaping it into a rising and falling movement for
each hexameter line.

## PART IV: LEARNING THE RHYTHM[10]

As indicated in Part III, the basic pattern or scheme of Greek and Latin metres is one of 'quantity', that is, of long and short syllables. The stressing of some of these syllables, which is called the beat or 'ictus', gives us the *rhythm* of the metre. However, this does not mean that one needs first to work out all the longs and shorts in a line, and then to go on to work out the rhythm. It is best to go straight for the rhythm; but in order to follow it, it is necessary to be able to recognise a long syllable and a short syllable at sight.

*Longs and Shorts: Rules for Syllable Quantity*[11]

The quantity of a syllable depends on two things: on the length of its vowel, and on what comes after that vowel. There are three possible situations:

1.  A syllable containing a long vowel or a diphthong is long, e.g. *ferae saxī dēiectae* (Specimen text line 2).

2.  A syllable containing a short vowel followed by not more than one consonant is short - that is, where a short vowel is *either* separated from the next vowel by one consonant, *or* is followed immediately by another vowel but without forming a diphthong.

It should be noted that *h* is not counted as a consonant in Latin; also that *i* and *u* standing before a vowel within the same syllable = the consonants *y* and *w* (except in *qu-* and *gu-* where the *u* should be disregarded - see Pronunciation Checklist); finally that *x* counts as two consonants = *ks*, e.g. *ĕccĕ fĕrae sāxī dēiēctae uĕrtĭcĕ cāprae* (specimen text line 2).

3.  A syllable containing a short vowel followed by more than one consonant (or *x*, see above) is long.[12]

The last syllable of a word is often long because of a second consonant beginning the *next* word, as in: *āt pŭĕr*. Where the second of two consonants after a short vowel is *l* or *r*, the syllable can count as long or as short. So we have: *cāprae* (specimen text line 2), but *ōptăt ăprum* (specimen text line 9).

*Practice with syllable length may be useful at this point. The reader is recommended firstly to go through lines 2, 3 and 5 (not 4) of the specimen text, checking each syllable to see which type it belongs to, and why; secondly to go through lines 10, 11, 13 and 14 (not 12), of the specimen*

22

*text, identifying each syllable as either long or short, with
the last syllable of the line always counting as long (see
note 5.)*

*The aim is to reach the point where you are identifying
syllables as long or short at sight, checking if in doubt
by referring to the definitions of the three types given
above.*

*Vowel-junctions*

Where one word ends with a vowel and the next word begins
with a vowel we have a vowel-junction (marked with the hyphen -).

There are three things to note:

1.  *h* does not count as a consonant in Latin; therefore,
where one word ends with a vowel, and the next word begins
with an *h*, we have a vowel-junction, as in the specimen
text line 6: *iamque-hos.*

2.  Where *m* ends a word, and the next word begins with a
vowel, the *m* is not a consonant, but nasalises the vowel
before it; therefore, where final *-am*, *-em*, *-im*, *-om* and
*-um* are followed by an initial vowel (or *h*), we have a
vowel-junction, e.g. twice in specimen text line 1: *postquam-altos uentum-in montis atque-inuia lustra.*

3.  *i* and *u* standing before a vowel within the same syllable =
the consonants *y* and *w*; therefore, where one word ends in
a vowel (or *m*), and the next begins with *i* or *u*, these *may*
be consonants and, if so, there is no vowel-junction.  In
the specimen text, compare: *atque-inuia* (line 1) with *equo
iamque = yamque* (line 7); and *inertia uotis = inertia wotis*
(line 8) with *summoque-ulul.arunt* (line 18).

Latin speakers, it seems, experienced a 'gap' or *hiatus* when
passing from one vowel to another *between* words.  The rules
of Latin verse are clearly meant to eliminate this phenomenon,
except at the line-end (and as an occasional exception within the line).[13]

At a vowel-junction the rule is to elide or 'knock out' the
first of the two vowels, that is, the vowel ending the first
word.  This rule must be uniformly applied to produce the
right sequence of long and short syllables required by the
metre in those lines - and they are many - which contain
vowel-junctions.  The specimen text has them in 10 lines
out of 22, namely lines 1, 4, 7, 8, 9, 12, 16, 17, 18, 20.
And note that there can be two and even three vowel-junctions
in one line, as in line 1.

At this stage, it will be best to read all vowel-junctions in the same way, uniformly dropping the first vowel, in accordance with the rule. We shall sometimes have the feeling that words are being mutilated by the loss of their final vowel, and that the sense sometimes becomes difficult to follow *by ear* as a result. It seems that we have to look beyond the basic rule, as given above, for an authentic pronunciation of these vowel-junctions. The subject is discussed in Appendix III, and in Part VII it will be suggested when might be a good time to consider adopting a more flexible pronunciation of vowel-junctions. What matters at this stage is that we should recognise a vowel-junction when we see one, and should discount the first vowel as we move from syllable to syllable along the line. So in line 1 of the specimen text, the syllable sequence required by the metre is: *post-qual-tos-uen-tin-mon-tis-at-quin-ui-a-lus-tra.*

*To practice the vowel-junction the reader should proceed as follows:*

*1.   Go through lines 1-14 of the specimen text, checking that all vowel-junctions have been duly marked.*

*2.   Go through lines 1-5, checking the sequence of long and short syllables as before, but now also discounting the first vowel at any vowel-junction. Again, it should be clear to you why each syllable is long or short, i.e. to which of the three types given at the beginning of this Part it belongs.*

*3.   Go on to lines 6-14, identifying each syllable as either long or short as before, but now also discounting the first vowel at every vowel-junction as you come to it. Again, if in doubt about the quantity of any syllable, check it with reference to the definitions of the three types given at the beginning of this Part.*

*4.   Go through lines 15-22, marking the vowel-junctions.*

*5.   Finally, repeat step 3 for lines 15-22.*

*The Varying Pattern of the Hexameter Line*

We saw in Parts II and III that the hexameter is a sequence of long and short syllables, organised around six beats or 'ictuses' and a mid-line division or caesura'. So far, in Part IV, we have been concerned with the identifying of syllables as either long or short - not forgetting to take account of vowel-junctions. We are now ready to master the actual pattern of the rhythm, with its play of variation on that fixed ground-plan of six ictuses and a caesura. What is not fixed is, first, what separates one ictus from the next and, second, the position of the caesura (see note 9): here there is, in each case, a choice between two

alternatives. What we need in order to read the hexameter
line is to recognise each ictus as we come to it, noting
the caesura as we pass.

*The Six Ictuses*

There are three useful rules to remember:

A. Every ictus falls on a long syllable; but not every
long syllable carries an ictus.

B. Short syllables *never* carry an ictus, and *always*
appear in pairs (except as the last syllable of the line;
see note 5).

C. Each ictus is separated from the next by *either* a
long syllable that has *no* ictus; or two short syllables,
without ictus of course. It is impossible for two adjacent
syllables both to carry an ictus.

*The reader should proceed as follows. First he should test
the first two of these rules, A and B, on the first five lines
of the specimen text. Then, noting that the first ictus
always falls on the first syllable, which is always long,
he should test the third rule, C, on the syllables separating
the first ictus from the second in each of the first five
lines of the specimen text. Finally, he should go through
the entire five lines, checking that all the ictuses have
been correctly marked. The following process may be helpful
in determining where the stresses fall :-*

*1. The first stress will be on the first syllable.*

*2. The following syllable is either a long syllable without
ictus (rules A and C above), and so the next syllable must
also be long, and carry the second ictus; or it is the first
of two shorts, both without ictus of course (rules B and C
above), and so the next syllable after these two shorts must
be long, and carry the second ictus.*

*3. The third, fourth and fifth ictuses may be determined in
the same manner. With the fifth ictus the beginning of the
cadence (see Part III above) is reached, with its fixed pattern of fifth foot dactyl (long-short-short) and sixth foot
spondee (long-long; see note 8).*

Of the six ictuses, then, the first always falls on the first
syllable, the sixth always falls on the last syllable but one,
and the fifth almost always three syllables before the sixth.
It turns out that it is the second, third and fourth ictuses
that are really subject to variation.

Finally, two important observations. First, the six feet

(see Part III) emerge of themselves as a by-product, so to
speak, of locating the six ictuses: each ictus begins a
foot. This can be checked by studying lines 1-14 of the
specimen text. Second, although we are proceeding, for
the moment, simply to stress according to the metre, it
is worth remembering that these six ictuses must interact
with the stresses of natural word-accent (see Part VII).
As with the pronouncing of vowel-junctions, so here too the
rules of the metre are not the whole story.


*The Caesura or Mid-line Division (see note 9)*

The rule is that every hexameter has a caesura at a word-
junction, i.e. between two words, immediately after the
third ictus; if there is no word-junction at that point,
the caesura falls immediately after the fourth ictus instead.[14]

The caesura gives the line a two-part movement, first rising,
then falling. How this interacts with the natural flow of
the sense will be our concern in Part V. Here again, the
rules of the metre are only part of the story; and here too
we should bear this in mind, as we proceed for the moment
simply to read according to the metre, registering a slight
break at the caesura without regard to the natural grouping
of words by their grammar or meaning.

*The reader should go through lines 6-22 of the specimen text,
checking that all caesuras are rightly marked (for line 16,
see note 15) and noticing in lines 10-22 how the sense-pauses
within the line (marked / or //) do not coincide with the
caesura.*


*The whole line*

*For practice with the whole line the reader is recommended
firstly to go through lines 6-14 again, this time checking
the six ictuses and the caesura in one continuous operation;
and secondly to read through the same lines, taking one line
at a time, with a strong rhythm - as he did in Part I, but
now with a sense of knowing what is going on. There should be
a stress at each ictus, a slight pause at each caesura, and
the sense-pauses marked in lines 10-14 should be ignored.
The stress should not be overdone and, in particular, the
voice should not be dropped at the caesura, or even at the
line-end, except at a full stop.*

# PART V: PHRASING - The Interplay of Meaning and Metre

Phrasing is an integral element of speech. It is the grouping of words by the use of pauses, and of variations in the pitch or intonation, the up-and-down movement, of the voice. In ordinary speech, phrasing is a matter of grouping the words according to their meaning into certain units and sub-units (sentences, clauses, etc.).[16] In poetry, the metre introduces another unit of its own, over and above the sense-units, namely, the verse or line; and in the hexameter (as in some other metres) there is also the sub-unit of the half-line. In reading Vergil, therefore, it is necessary to phrase the text both according to its meaning and according to the metre, in a kind of dynamic interplay.

## Pauses

There are two broad types of pause: *a major pause* is a break in continuity, involving the sense of coming to a stop and making a fresh start; *a minor pause* is a suspension or delay, which does not break the continuity; it is a momentary lingering, but without the sense of stopping and starting afresh.

The difference between a major and minor pause is not simply a matter of duration. Major pauses do tend to be longer than minor ones (the total range here is wide, and the graduations within it very fine and very free). It is rather a matter of what is happening to the pitch of the voice. It maybe helpful here to think of the voice as tracing a wavy line of rising and falling pitch. At a major pause, one such line comes to an end, normally with a characteristic drop in pitch (some questions and exclamations, and some kinds of emphasis, end on an 'up' rather than a 'down'); and, after a shorter or longer interval, a new line begins. By contrast, at a minor pause the voice adjusts it pitch-line in such a way as to make the pause, whatever its duration, feel provisional rather than final. Instead of separating the end of one pitch-line from the beginning of the next one, it is a hesitation or suspension of one such pitch-line during its progress. The key to getting this right in reading is to avoid dropping the voice (as at a major pause), but to keep it up during this momentary lingering.

## Phrasing and Punctuation

The phrasing of speech is a very subtle phenomenon, partly fixed and uniform, partly free and individual. Yet the distinction between a major and minor pause, between break and

suspension, remains basic.  This is related to our system of
punctuation, whether in English or in printed Latin texts.

Broadly speaking, all major punctuation marks - that is,
all except the comma (and sometimes dashes and brackets) -
indicate a major pause.  It would be very convenient if we
would rely on the comma to indicate every minor pause.  In
fact, however, a comma is sometimes placed where there is a
definite (major) break in continuity, and sometimes no
comma is placed where we have a suspension.  In reading
Vergil, then, it is necessary certainly to take full account
of the editor's punctuation (it is not Vergil's, of course),
but it must be remembered all the time that it is an incomplete and, to that extent, sometimes a misleading guide to
phrasing.

## The Line-end

In reading Vergil, the text should be phrased quite naturally
acccording to its meaning, registering each major and minor
pause.  But, in addition, the metre requires that the reader
register its own minor (suspensive) pause at the end of
every line.  Two points about the line-end should be noted:
firstly, there is a pause at the end of *every line*;  and secondly;
this pause is  a minor or suspensive one, a slight lingering
with the voice kept up - unless, of course, it coincides
with a major sense-pause.

## End-stopped Lines and Run-on Lines (Enjambement)

There are three possible situations in the interplay of
meaning and metre at the line-end:

*either* the end of the line coincides with a major sense-
pause  - an end-stopped line, the metre and the meaning re-
inforcing one another with a strong and satisfying feeling
of completion;

*or* the sense runs straight on over the end of the line and
into the next  - a run-on line (another term used is the
French word *enjambement*, from *enjamber* 'to straddle'; it
gives a picture of the sense straddling across the gap
between one line and the next).  Here the metre pulls
against the meaning, by requiring a perceptible suspension
(but *not* a break) where the meaning has none.  There is a
tension, which preserves the felt presence of the metre, yet
without reverting to a monotonous line-by-line recitation;

*or* the end of the line coincides with a minor, rather than
a major pause in the sense.  Such a line is assimilated to
one or other of the two types above; either the metre reinforces the pause, and it becomes a major one; or else

it becomes indistinguishable from an *enjambement*.

The reader may find it useful at this point to go through lines 10-22 of the specimen text, checking that the right type of pause has been assigned to each line-end.


*Internal or Mid-line Pauses*

Vergil has ensured that sense-pauses occur as much, indeed perhaps more, *within* the line than at the line-end. These internal pauses may be minor ones, as in line 17 of the specimen text after *ignes*, and again in line 18; often they are major ones, as in lines 14, 16, 17 and 20. All these internal pauses arise from the sense, not from the metre; and it is to some extent a matter of judgement whether a pause is present at any given point and, if so, of which kind it is. Vergil is fond of lines with *no* internal pauses (lines 10, 12, 15, 19 and 21; but see note 16).

Three favourite positions for pauses within the line are: after 2nd ictus; after 3rd ictus; after 4th ictus. Of the other possibilities, Vergil uses some more than others, with a good sprinkling of unusual ones to defeat expectation - as in lines 14 and 22 of the specimen text.[17] Nor can we predict relative distribution in any given passage: in lines 10-22 there is not one instance of a sense-pause after the 3rd ictus.

*The reader may find it useful here to check that every mid-line pause in lines 10-22 has been duly marked, and is of the right kind.*


*The Caesura: the 'Shadow' of a Pause in the Metre?*

The pauses we have just been considering arise from the *sense*: they would be there equally if the text were prose, not verse. How then do they interact with the caesura required by the *metre*? As seen in Part IV, the hexameter is divided into two parts after the third ictus (or after the fourth if, and only if, there is no word-junction after the third). In reading the line, we have been content to treat the caesura as an actual minor pause in mid-line, regardless of the sense. This gave the caesura the same status in the metre as the line-end itself, where indeed the metre does introduce a minor pause of its own, independent of the sense. Not so at the caesura: this metrical division is weaker than the line-end, and does not amount to a minor pause in its own right. In a sense, the most important thing to remember about the caesura in reading is *not* to pause there if there is no sense-pause. To register a clear pause over and above the sense-pauses in the middle of every line as well as at its end would intolerably disrupt

the flow of the sense, and where there is no coinciding
sense-pause the caesura may be ignored in our reading.

Why then does the hexameter regularly have a caesura? It
may be that a very fine recording instrument would in fact
register a tiny pause at this point in each line. Or else
we can suppose that sheer familiarity with the metre produces
an inward impression of the words grouping themselves into
two half-lines. Be that as it may, the caesura represents
something much less than a minor pause, yet which can perhaps be described as the 'shadow' of a pause at that point
in the line; or as a very slight pull on the reader to pause,
though much weaker than at the line-end. When this pull coincides with a natural sense-break, then the reader should
pause there, and should do so with an added sense of an
expectation fulfilled (like that at the line-end, when it
coincides with a break in the sense). Without such a
sense-break, the line runs on without pausing, for the
caesura is not strong enough to hold it back: but it still
registers on our inward ear, as an expectation unfulfilled,
and most strongly so in lines that are continuous and have
no internal sense-pause.

The symbol ⁝ well represents the subtle and unobtrusive
presence of the caesura, in contrast to the more substantial
/ of a minor pause. However, if all this proves *too* subtle,
the caesura can safely be ignored in reading; or rather,
it can be left to develop its own subtle impact on the
inward ear as the metre becomes familiar. This does mean
that the slight pause used to register the caesura in Part IV
must now be given up. It served its purpose of making the
reader conscious of the hexameter line as a two-part structure.

*The reader is now recommended to read through lines 6-22 of*
*the specimen text, inwardly registering each caesura as*
*marked, but now without pausing.*


*Continuous Phrasing*

The use of *enjambement* at the line-end, the varied sense-
pauses in mid-line, and the 'shadow' or pull of the caesura
- these together create the dynamic interplay of meaning and
metre in hexameter poetry. It is worth considering for a
moment how monotonous it would be if the poem consisted
entirely of end-stopped lines, with either no internal
pauses, or with a pause at every caesura. Indeed, we can
actually experience something of this monotony in a poem
by Catullus, though it is beautiful in many ways: the
marriage hymn for Peleus and Thetis (poem 64). Vergil
exhibits, here as elsewhere, an instinct for realising
the full potential of his medium, in a perfect balance
between variety and predictability.

In order to grasp each of the three elements firmly - the
line-end, the sense-pauses in mid-line, and the caesura -
it is natural at first to concentrate on one line at a
time, treating it as a self-contained unit. It now remains to join up the lines into a continuous reading.

*The whole process may be taken in three steps, using the
last two sections of the specimen text:-*

*1.   The Line-end, where the reader should take the text
one line at a time, concentrating only on the line-end,
at a major pause registering a break, normally with some
drop in the tone of voice and at a minor pause registering
a slight lingering or hesitation, with the voice kept up.*

*2.   Internal Pauses and Caesura, where the reader should
still read each line as a self-contained unit, this time
concentrating on the internal pauses, while also sensing
the 'shadow' or pull of the caesura.  In this way the difference between a continuous, uninterrupted line, with
the slight pull near its centre, and a line interrupted by
an internal pause, should clearly emerge.*

*3.   Continuous Reading, where the final task is to join
up the lines into a continuous reading.  Phrasing is to some
extent a matter of nuance and judgment, and does not always
emerge line by line, but only when the movement of the sense
over several lines can be taken into account - which implies
that a perfect reading must be a prepared reading.*[18] *It is
worth noting that enjambement makes it possible to build
continuous units (i.e. without a major pause) of two lines
and upwards.  The reader should attempt to convey this.*

In Vergil this effect will usually be in some way reinforc-
ing or bringing out the meaning conveyed by the words.  So
in lines 12-14 of the specimen text, the unchecked movement,
with all those rapid dactyls, that runs on over two and half
lines and even then cannot check itself in time for the break
to be in a predictable position - all this vividly conveys
the hunting party fleeing in sheer panic before the uncanny
storm.

Vergil's poetry falls naturally into sections, or periods,
rather like paragraphs (as shown in the specimen text).
These sections divide into sub-sections, and combine into
episodes - but this is to move out of the realm of phrasing
into that of performance.  Nevertheless, to phrase sensi-
tively, we need to remember that every line belongs to a
larger grouping of lines - end-stopped lines no less than
run-on lines.  The major pause at the end of a section will
surely be longer than others, and the completion of the
pitch-line more decisive than at other major pauses (one
might even use a triple /// to mark the end of a section).

Such refinements can be left to take care of themselves.

The crucial requirement of phrasing is to register the pauses, and to distinguish between the break of a major pause and the suspension of a minor one - and to sense the 'shadow' or pull of the caesura - within a natural, continuous reading.

## PART VI: FROM MARKED TEXT TO READING AT SIGHT

*Further practice on the specimen text:* so far, in this
booklet that text has been used to supply a ready-made
sample of each of the five features of the verse which have
been dealt with: vowel-junctions (sections 1, 2 and 3: lines
1-14); long and short syllables (section 1: lines 1-5); the
six ictuses (sections 1, 2 and 3: lines 1-14); the caesura
(sections 2, 3 and 4: lines 6-22); and phrasing - major and
minor pauses (sections 3 and 4: lines 10-22).

None of the four sections of the specimen text in fact marks
all five features, and it can therefore be used as practice
for putting in the other markings: vowel-junctions (section
4: lines 15-22); long and short syllables (sections 2, 3
and 4: lines 6-22);the six ictuses (section 4: lines 15-22);
the caesura (section 1: lines 1-5); and phrasing - major
and minor pauses (sections 1 and 2: lines 1-9).

*The following sequence may be found helpful. Two copies of
the specimen text, version A, will be needed, one to mark
and the other to be left as it stands. If practice with
identifying vowel-junctions or longs and shorts is still
required, begin with Step 1; otherwise with Step 2. The
marking of longs and shorts is not an aid for actually
reading the verse, but only for locating the six ictuses
of each line. For actual reading the aids are three: the
six ictuses; the caesura; and the pauses, major and minor.*

Step 1:    Long and Short syllables; Vowel Junctions.

(a)    *Check all the vowel-junctions of sections 1-3, then
mark those of section 4 (there are four of them): throughout,
consult the rule given in Part IV.*

(b)    *Read over section 1 of the specimen text, making sure
that you see why each syllable is marked long or short,
according to the rules given in Part IV.*

(c)    *With these rules still before you, go through the lines
of sections 2 and 3 (but not 4), marking each syllable as
long or short.*

(d)    *Turn to the method given in Part IV for locating the
six ictuses, and check that your new markings for longs
and shorts agree with the six ictuses already marked in
these lines.*

(e)    *Take your second copy of the specimen text, and read
through the lines of sections 2 and 3, identifying each
syllable as either long or short in your mind. At first,*

*keep checking your choice against your own markings on
the other copy. Gradually, you will find that you can
identify them more and more accurately without the markings.*

(f)     *Finally, when you are ready, test your confidence by
working through section 4 without markings.*

Step 2: The Six Ictuses

(a)     *Without first marking longs and shorts, go through
section 4 and mark the six ictuses in each line, according
to the method given in Part IV.*

(b)     *With this method still before you, take your second
copy of the text, and go through section 4, locating the
six ictuses in your mind. At first, keep checking your
choices against your own markings on the other copy. Continue until this checking has become superfluous.*

Step 3: The Caesura

(a)     *Go through section 1, marking the caesura in each
line, according to the rules given in Part IV.*

(b)     *With these rules still before you, take your second
copy of the text and go through section 1 locating the
caesura in each line. At first, check your choices against
the markings on the other copy, until this becomes superfluous.*

Step 4: Phrasing - Major and Minor Pauses

(a)     *Go through sections 1 and 2, marking the major and
minor pauses in each line, according to the principles given
in Part V.*

(b)     *With these principles still before you, take your second
copy of the text, and go through sections 1 and 2, phrasing
the lines as you read. At first, check your pauses, major
and minor, against your markings on the other copy. Gradually
you will get used to phrasing quite naturally, without any
markings.*

Step 5: Continuous reading of the fully marked text (omitting
lines 1-5, which are cluttered with the now unnecessary longs
and shorts)

(a)     *Take the copy with your own markings on it, and read
over lines 6-22. As you read, register the markings in*

*your mind and with your voice - the six ictuses; the*
*caesuras;the (major and minor) pauses.*

(b)  *Now go back to the specimen text in its original*
*form.  Read through lines 6-22 again: section 3 already*
*has all three kinds of markings, but in section 2 you will*
*be supplying the pauses in your mind, and likewise the*
*ictuses in section 4.  You have in fact already been doing*
*this in previous 'steps', but this time it should be hap-*
*pening as part of a sustained, continuous reading - and*
*now, if not before, aloud.*

(c)  *Keep going over these same lines until their rhythm*
*and phrasing feel familiar and secure.*

(d)  *Finally, find this text (Aeneid IV, 151-72) in an*
*ordinary printed text of Vergil.  Read through the passage*
*in this text.  Your mind, and voice, should now reproduce*
*the rhythm and phrasing without any markings, though it*
*may be necessary to continue practising until you feel that*
*you can read (and speak) the plain printed lines with a full*
*sense of their rhythm and phrasing.*


*Marking a Plain Text*

It should now be possible for the reader to choose any
passage from Vergil and mark it from scratch, using a method
virtually the same as that outlined in the specimen text
above.  (Two copies will be needed if starting from Step
1 below, one if starting from Step 2.)  When Step 3 is
completed the marked text will look like section 3 of the
specimen text.  A passage from *Aeneid* 6 is used as a sample
in what follows.


Step 1: Long and Short syllables

(Marking longs and shorts is *not* part of marking a text for
reading, but a preparation for it.  If you feel fairly confident about recognising a long and a short syllable, proceed
straight away to Step 2.)

(a)  *Take one copy of the chosen text, and work through it*
*line by line, marking first any vowel-junctions there may*
*be, and then every syllable as either long or short, accord-*
*ing to the rules given in Part IV; e.g.* Aeneid 6.847-8:

excūdent ălĭĭ spīrāntĭă mōllĭŭs aĕra
(crēdo-ĕquĭdēm), uĭuōs dūcēnt dē mārmŏrĕ uūltūs,

(b)  *Go through the marked text and add markings for the six*
*ictuses and the caesura in each line, according to the pro-*
*cedure given in Part IV; this will automatically involve*

*checking your longs and shorts:*

excūdent ălĭi ː spīrantĭă mollĭŭs aērā
(crēdo ĕquĭdem), uĭuŏs ː dūcent dē marmŏrĕ uūltūs,

(c)    *Read through the same lines in the plain printed
text, mentally registering the sequence of longs and
shorts, the position of the six ictuses and the caesura:*

excudent alii spirantia mollius aera

(credo equidem), uiuos ducent de marmore uultus,

*When this feels reasonably secure, you are ready to do the
same thing without first marking out the longs and shorts.*


Step 2: The Six Ictuses and the Caesura

(It is worth repeating here that it is not necessary first
to mark out the longs and the shorts before marking the
line for rhythmic reading.  On the contrary, longs and
shorts clutter the text, and distract attention from the
rhythm - whereas the whole object of the exercise is to become so familiar with the rhythm, by the aid of these markings, that we can then dispense with them and pick out the
rhythm of each line at sight.)

(a)    *Given that you can identify each syllable as long or
short as you come to it, go through the copy of the text,
marking each line with the sequence of six ictuses and a
caesura (for the rules, see Part IV); e.g. Aeneid 6.849:*

orábunt causás ː melĭus, caelíque meátus

*Read over the marked lines, preferably aloud, until the
rhythm feels thoroughly familiar.*

(b)    *Now turn to the plain printed text, and read through
the same lines, picking out the sequence of the six ictuses
and the caesura in your mind - and with your voice.  Check
your reading against your marked copy as necessary, until
you can dispense with the latter entirely and still read
with a full and ready sense of rhythm:*

orabunt causas melius, caelique meatus


Step 3: Phrasing - Major and Minor pauses

(As indicated in Part V, phrasing is partly a matter of fixed
requirements, partly a matter of nuance and judgment.  The
requirements are three: (a) the minor pause required by the
metre at the end of every line, regardless of the sense; (b)

the major pause required by the sense at a full stop or
equivalent (semi colon, question mark etc.), whether this
occurs at the line-end of in mid-line; (c) the 'shadow' or
pull of the caesura. Beyond these three requirements, however,
it is necessary to sense where pauses occur, and of what kind
they are; this cannot always happen line by line, but results
from an awareness of the whole movement of the sense.)

(a)   *Having marked a natural section, or group of lines,
with the six ictuses and the caesura, mark a minor pause
at each line-end, and a major pause at every full stop or
equivalent.  Read through the lines, aloud, registering
the pauses (as well as the rhythm) as marked;* e.g. Aeneid
6.847-53:

excúdent álii : spirántia móllius áëra /
(crédo equídem), uíuos : dúcent de mármore uúltus, /
orábunt cáusas : mélius, caelíque méatus /
descríbent rádio ét : surgéntia sídera dícent: //
tú régere império : pópulos, Rómane, meménto /
(háe tíbi erúnt ártes), : pacíque impónere mórem, /
párcere subíectis : et débelláre supérbos. //

(b)   *Read through the lines again; see whether any line-end
needs a major rather than a minor pause because of the
sense; introduce any internal pauses within the line, major
or minor, as required by the sense.  This is to some extent
subjective and one reader's version might be different from
another's:* e.g. Aeneid 6.847-53:

excúdent álii : spirántia móllius áëra /
(crédo equídem), // uíuos : dúcent de mármore uúltus, /
orábunt cáusas : mélius, / caelíque méatus /
descríbent rádio / ét : surgéntia sídera dícent: //
tú régere império : pópulos, / Rómane, meménto /
(háe tíbi erúnt ártes) :, / pacíque impónere mórem, /
párcere subíectis : / et débelláre supérbos. //

(c)   *When you are satisfied, read over your marked text,
always maintaining the rhythm, until the phrasing too feels
thoroughly familiar.*

(d)   *Now turn to the plain printed text, and read through the
same lines, picking out the rhythm and the phrasing in your
mind, and with your voice.  Check your reading against your
marked copy as necessary, until you can dispense with it -
that is, until you find that the plain text generates the
rhythm and the phrasing for you as you go along:*

excudent alii spirantia mollius aera
(credo equidem), uiuos ducent de marmore uultus,
orabunt causas melius, caelique meatus
describent radio et surgentia sidera dicent:
tu regere imperio populos, Romane, memento
(hae tibi erunt artes), pacique imponere morem,
parcere subiectis et debellare superbos.

## From Marked Text to Reading at Sight

Gradually, the marking of a text as described above becomes
quicker and quicker, and the transfer of the marked pattern
of rhythm and phrasing to the same text in plain print
becomes easier and easier, until the marking stage can be
omitted altogether, and the reader can come to Vergil and
read at sight a normal printed text, with a full sense of
rhythm and phrasing.

PART VII: ICTUS AND ACCENT - The Interplay of Verse-beat
                and Word-accent


    So far we have read Vergil's hexameter poetry according
to the rhythm of its metre.  This of course involves giving
some of the words an unnatural stress.  So for instance in
line 1 of the specimen text the metre stresses: *post tos in
tis in lus*; whereas the natural accents fall on: *post al
uen mon in lus*.  But if we believe that words bring their
natural accents with them, in Latin as in English, when
they take their place in a line of poetry, then we can see
that the interplay between verse-beat and word-accent could
be a subtle but powerful element in the life of the poetry.

The idea that ictus and accent interact in Latin, as they do
in English, is now well established, and forms the basis of
much senstive appreciation of Vergil's poetry.  Yet to be
authentic this interaction must be something that can be
realised in actual reading.  No doubt English readers of
Latin poetry have sensed it subconsciously, even when they
actually read the lines by 'drumming out' the metre, as we
have been doing so far in this booklet; or when they preferred to ignore the metre and read the words naturally as in
prose.  The problem is quite simply stated: how can we read
a word with its natural accent intact, and at the same time
also stress another syllable in that word because it carries
the ictus?


*Varying Stress*

In ordinary speech we stress words on a particular syllable
(sometimes two) and leave the others unstressed.  But we
vary the amount of energy we put into our stressing: it is
one of the ways in which we give more importance or emphasis
to some words than to others.  What about the verse-beat,
the stressing by which we produce the rhythm of a metre?

Let us take the opening lines of Shakespeare's *Twelfth Night*.
Its metre (sometimes called the iambic pentameter) is the
traditional line of English blank verse, consisting of ten
syllables with five stresses, on alternate syllables beginning on the second.  The lines should first be read just as
they are marked, with a smooth and relaxed sense of the
rhythm:

            If music be the food of love, play on,
            give me excess of it; that, surfeiting,
            the appetite may sicken and so die.

We find that the rhythm produces an unvarying, even monotonous, up-and-down movement from syllable to syllable
throughout the line, and from line to line.

As prose, the passage would probably be stressed like this:

If músic be the foód of lóve, pláy ón, gíve me excéss
of it; that, súrfeiting, the áppetite may sícken and
só díe.

We notice that there is no pattern about these word-accents,
which can be far apart or next to each other in a way quite
different from the verse-beat; and some of them are clearly
stronger than others, unlike the even monotony of the verse-
beat.

If we put the two, verse-beat and word-accent, together, the
passage becomes:

If music be the food of love, play on
give me excess of it; that, surfeiting,
the appetite may sicken and so die

The two kinds of stress sometimes fall on the same syllable,
sometimes on different ones - sometimes coincide, sometimes
alternate.[19] Imagine yourself reading over these lines into a
sensitive recording instrument which registers the variations
in the energy level of your voice, on a four-point scale. It
readings might be:

1. Syllables with no marking: minimum energy
2. Syllables with ictus only: an unvarying moderate stress
3. Syllables with accent only: a varying stress, but with an
   average energy level higher than that of the ictus
4. Syllables with coincidence of ictus and accent: a strong
   stress.

*Coincidence and Alternation*

The hexameter is certainly more complex than English blank
verse, but the principle remains the same. It may be helpful
here to think of the hexameter line as a chain of syllables,
along which pass two simultaneous waves of stress energy. One
is the undulation of the verse-beat: it has a fixed number of
six peaks (the six ictuses), all of the same height, and
separated from each other by troughs that admit of just one
variation, being either of one long syllable or two short ones.
The overall energy of this wave is only moderate, and quite
constant. The other undulation is that set up by the sequence
of all the word-accents in the line: it has five or six peaks,

occasionally seven,[20] and its troughs too are much more
variable (two accents can even be adjacent). Its energy-
level or pulse, varies constantly, according as some words
are naturally stressed more than others, but overall it is
stronger than that of the verse-beat. As these two waves
pass along the syllable chain, their peaks will either
coincide on the same syllable, giving it a high peak of
stress; or they will alternate on adjacent syllables, two or
more up to seven, giving them a sustained lift or swell. In
this swell, the accents remain a little higher than the ictuses; but an ictus does give a syllable more stress than it
would have in prose, and the whole sequence rises clearly
higher than the unstressed syllables in the line. The result
is an enhanced pronunciation of words in verse, more deliberate and intense than that of prose.

As an example, let us take *Aeneid* 1.588:

Restitit Aeneas : claraque-in luce refulsit

There stood Aeneas, and shone out in brilliant light

Here coincidence gives three strong peaks, while alternation
gives a sustained swell over five syllables in which -*re*- and
*cla*- retain their natural dominance, but *Ae*- -*as* and -*ra*-
carry more energy than the unstressed syllables -*titit*-, *in*
etc., and more energy than they would themselves carry in
prose. The alternation in lines 1, 4, 15 16 and 21 of the
specimen text sustains a continuous swell over the first
half of the line, even though no coincidence occurs.


*The Cadence Again: from Tension to Resolution.*

A glance at the specimen text (version B), sections 2 and 3,
will show that the cadence, with which we are already familiar,
regularly requires coincidence of the last two ictuses and the
last two accents in the line.[21] This required 'double'
cadence is on occasions extended to cover the last three
ictuses and accents in the line, giving a 'triple' cadence:
Vergil particularly likes it for ending a section, as in lines
9, 18 and 22 of the specimen text. By contrast, there must be
at least one instance of alternation in the first part of every
line, and overall it is here predominant. During alternation,
the rhythm or pulse of the metre is lost, but its evergy is
felt in the lift or swell already noted; the pulse always re-
turns strongly with the cadence. Before the first stroke of
the cadence, double or triple, there is normally a kind of
lull, consisting of a foot free of word-accent,[22] e.g.

... alia de parte patentis (double cadence, line 3), and

... insequitur commixta grandine nimbus (triple cadence, line 11)
The overall movement of the hexameter is thus from a certain
tension in the first part to a resolution in the second.[23]

*The Name Aeneas: a Glimpse of Vergil at Work?*

We come now to a fascinating observation. Words of three long
syllables, like *Aeneas*, can fit into the hexameter in two ways.
They can either carry one ictus coinciding with the accent on
their middle syllable; or they can carry two ictuses, one
either side of their accent. Contrast, for instance, from the
specimen text, *deiectae* (line 2), and *transmittunt* (line 4).
In the first version, the prose pronunciation of the word is
retained and even reinforced, with *de-* and *-tae* spoken 'flat'
at the minimum energy level, and a strong peak of stress on
*-iec-*. In the latter version, the middle syllable *-mit-* re-
tains its dominance; but *trans-* and *-tunt*, instead of remaining 'flat' as in prose, are lifted by the ictus as high as they
can rise without challenging the dominance of *-mit-*. The whole
word has a deliberate, sonorous intensity , perceptibly
different from its sound in prose.[24]

Now the name *Aeneas* could appear in either of these arrange-
ments. We could have either *Aeneas*, as in the line quoted
above (*Aeneid* 1.588):

estitit Aeneas : claraque-in luce refulsit

Or we could have *Aeneas*:

at pius exsequiis : Aeneas rite solutis (*Aen.*7.5.)

But pious Aeneas, having duly performed the funeral rites

In fact (so a computer search will now quickly reveal!),this line from
Book 7 is the only instance in the poem of the second arrangement. This
does seem to suggest that Vergil was sensitive to the difference, and was exercising an overwhelming preference for the enhancement
of his hero's name by the sustained swell. The counterpoint between
ictus and accent therefore seems to be something real and authentic.
There also seems to be something deeply and authentically Roman
here, in the sheer sense of sustained force or power generated in
the words themselves, whose heavy, slow intensity gives them the
flavour of the great 'Roman virtues': *grauitas, temperantia,
constantia, fortitudo*,and *dignitas*. What gives this poetry its
comparable quality, however, is the combination of this sheer
power with such subtle sensitivity. Is that Roman too - or
is it uniquely Vergilian?

*Practising Word-accent*

The final stage in the correct pronunciation of the hexameter
is to learn to hear and speak the counterpoint of ictus and
accent. Being now reasonably fluent in the metre, it would
seem the obvious way of proceeding simply to mark both on a
text as in sections 2 and 3 of the specimen text. But since,
so far, we have been reading according to the metre and thus
stressing words unnaturally, it may be as well first to let

our ear dwell on the natural word-accents for a while, before
then going on to develop a feeling for their subtle interplay
with the verse-beat.

It will be helpful if our markings show visually the greater
energy carried by the word-accents. Alongside the little
vertical ' which we use to mark the ictus (and so also the
beginning of each foot), we should ensure that the slanting /
used for word-accent *looks* stronger, being either heavier
or longer. As for coincidence, the two markings can simply
be combined into a ✓, rather like a 'tick'.

On the whole, the English ear is a good guide to Latin
accentuation, always provided that we are pronouncing the Latin
word correctly, particularly in the matter of vowel-length:
wrong vowel-length ('false quantity') often also involves
accenting the wrong syllable.

*You will need two copies of the specimen text, version B.*


Step 1

*Read over lines 1-5 of the specimen text, stressing each word
as marked by the accent. Notice particularly any word that
sounds different from what you would have expected. Remember
that some short words may have no word-accent (see 'Rules for
Word-accent', Part IC above).*


Step 2

*Go through the same lines and check the accent on every word,
using the following sequence:*

1. Trisyllables, *applying the basic 'rule of the penultimate'.*

2. Disyllables, *remembering that those ending in a vowel-
   junction may be treated as monosyllables with an optional
   accent.*
   *N.B.: these five lines contain no example of a pyrrhic
   word of two short syllables, whose accent is optional
   like that of monosyllables, e.g. puer in line 6.*

3. Monosyllables. *Do you agree that all those occurring in
   these fives lines should be left unaccented?*

4. Polysyllables, *with their potential secondary accent.*


Step 3

*Go through lines 6-14 of the specimen text, reading the words
according to the word-accent only. Again, notice any word*

*whose sound surprises you.*

Step 4

*Go through the same nine lines, checking the accent on
every word, using the sequence suggested under Step 2 above.
This time you have no longs or shorts to show you why each
accent stands where it does. Make sure that you can see why
in each case; if necessary, mark longs and shorts yourself
on one copy of the specimen text.*

Step 5

*Go through lines 15-22, marking one copy of the specimen
text as follows:*

1.  *One accent on every word of* three *or more syllables,
    as required by the basic 'rule of the penultimate'.*

2.  *Accent all disyllables on their first syllable. Now check
    any pyrrhics of two short syllables and any ending in a
    vowel-junction, both of which types have an optional accent.*

3.  *Leave all monosyllables unaccented.*

4.  *Polysyllables, some of which carry a secondary accent.*

Step 6

*Read over lines 15-22 in your marked version, stressing the
accent.*

Step 7

*Now read over the same lines in the unmarked copy, stressing
the accents as you recall them, and using your marked copy as
a check when necessary, until you feel quite confident about
your accentuation.*

*The Pronunciation of Vowel-junctions*

We have now reached the point when we are seeking a more
authentic balance between ictus and accent, so it would seem
to be a good moment to look more closely at the pronunciation
of vowel-junctions. We saw in Part IV that the metre always
requires us to discount the *first* vowel at a vowel-junction
when we are counting syllables: this procedure is called
'elision' . So in line 1 of the specimen text, the syllables

are counted like this:

*post-qual-tos-uen-tin-mon-tis-at-quin-ui-a-lus-tra.*

Naturally enough, many readers have read the verse accordingly, just as they have also stressed simply according to
the metre like this:

*póstqu-altós uent-ín montís ! atqu-ínuia lústra.*

Then, however, just as some readers felt unhappy with the
way metrical stressing distorted the natural sound of many
words, so they also felt unhappy with the way uniform elision
mutilated many words by the loss of their final syllable,
especially when it is a long syllable (so-called 'heavy
elision'). It also seems often to make it harder for the ear
to follow the sense. So some readers now retain both vowels
at every vowel-junction, tolerating the resulting 'hiatus'
and the extra syllable for which the metre has no room; and
at the same time they tend to stress by word-accent alone,
so sacrificing the rhythm entirely (except in the cadence)
and reading the text as prose thus:

*póstquam áltos uéntum in móntis atque ínuia lústra*

There is some evidence that the Romans did not always
elide the first vowel at all vowel-junctions. Sometimes
they certainly elided the *second-vowel* instead, e.g. saying
(and writing) *bonumst* for *bonum est.* Within a word, they
sometimes ran together or *contracted* two vowels into a
single vowel or diphthong, e.g. *de-hinc* (spoken as two
syllables) into *deinc* (spoken as one). So why not contract
between two words also? Again, within a word, the first
of two vowels was sometimes turned into the *consonantal y*
or *w*, e.g. *an-te-hac* (spoken as three syllables) became
*antyac* (two syllables). So again, why not between two
words also? Finally, there remains the possibility, at times,
of *retaining both vowels* in full, against the metre, especially at a strong sense-pause. The whole subject is more fully
discussed in Appendix III.


*The Counterpoint of Ictus and Accent.*

In the cadence, of course, there is no problem: the accents
simply reinforce the familiar rhythm of the metre, line by
line. It is the first part of the line with which we shall
be concerned here. Using sections 2 and 3 of the specimen
text (version B), we can proceed as follows:

Step 8

(a)   *Read line 6 according to the metre, stressing the six ictuses, thus:*

At puer Áscaniùs : mediis in uállibus ácri.

(b)    *Read the words as prose, thus:*

At púer Ascánius médiis in uállibus ácri.

(c)    *Carefully practise the words which carry ictus and accent on separate syllables, dwelling on a syllable with ictus just a little more heavily than you would normally, but not enough to make this syllable sound stronger than the one carrying the accent, thus:  Ascániùs and médiis.*

(d)    *Now read over the line as marked on your copy, taking care that Ascanius and mediis sound as practised under (c).*


Step 9

(a)    *Read over line 7, stressing the six ictuses, thus:*

gaùdet equò iamque-hòs : cursù, iam praéterit íllos.

(b)    *Read the words as prose, thus:*

gaúdet équo iámque hós cúrsu, iam praéterit íllos.

(c)    *Carefully practise the words which carry ictus and accent on separate syllables, as suggested under 8(c) above:   équò and cúrsù.*

(d)    *Now read through the line as marked on your copy, taking care that equo and cursu sound as practised under (c).*


Step 10

(a)    *Read over lines 8-9, stessing the six ictuses, thus:*

spùmantémque darì : pecora-ìnter inértia uòtis

óptat aprum-aùt fuluùm : descéndere mònte leónem.

(b)    *Read the words as prose, thus:*

spúmantémque dári pécora ínter inértia uótis óptat áprum aut

fúluum descéndere mónte leónem.

(c)    *Carefully practise the words which carry both ictus and accent on separate syllables, as suggested under 8(c) above. Thus:   dárì and fúluùm.*

(d)   *Now read through the lines as marked on your copy, taking care that* dari *and* fuluum *sound as practised under (c).*

Step 11

*Read over lines 6-9 as a consecutive passage, taking care to retain the counterpoint on the words you have practised.*

Step 12

(a)   *Practise the same counterpoint on the following combination:*

At púer;   hós cúrsù;   dári pécora;   áprum-aùt fúluùm.

(b)   *Read lines 6-9 over again, observing the counterpoint on these combinations as well as on the individual words already worked through.*

Step 13

*Read through lines 10-14 as marked, to see how far the counterpoint is already registering in your mind.*

Step 14

*Now go through the same passage line by line, working out for yourself the sequence suggested in Steps 8-12 above.*

Step 15

*Now read through the same lines again:*

(a)   *first concentrating on the ictus-accent counterpoint alone;*

(b)   *and then also on the interplay of metre and meaning, as shown by the phrasing (caesuras and pauses).*

Further Practice on the Specimen Text (Version B), lines 15-22

Step 16

*On one of your two copies these lines have already been marked with accents, under Step 5 above: now mark the other copy with ictuses.  Read through the lines on each copy in turn, supplying in your mind the other kind of stress in each case.*

*Continue doing this, switching from one copy to the other,
until you feel your reading is the same on both copies, and
fairly fluent.*

Step 17

*Now go through both copies, marking the missing kind of
stress in each case, but without looking at the other copy.
Read over the fully marked lines with a confident sense of
the counterpoint of ictus and accent, and now also with a
sense of the interplay of metre and meaning in the phrasing
as marked (caesuras and pauses).*

Step 18

*Finally, turn to these lines where they actually appear in
version B on p. 8 . Read the lines over with a full sense
both of the counterpoint and of the phrasing. Use your
marked copy as a check when you feel uncertain, until you are
able to dispense with it altogether.*

*Marking a Text for Full Reading*

It would obviously be possible to take a passage of hexameter verse and go through it twice, marking first the metre
and then the accents (and perhaps a third time for the
pauses), and finally to practise reading the lines over.
After a while one could go back to the plain, unmarked
text, and read it confidently, with a real sense of all the
elements we have encountered. But if our aim is, eventually,
to register all these elements *as we come to them*, then we
need to practise marking ictus and accent together, word by
word, as we go through the line - adding marks for the phrasing as well, though (as we saw at the end of Part V) this
cannot be finalised until we re-read the passage as a whole.

Two points are helpful in following the ictuses and accents
simultaneously through the line:

1. *The First Part of the Line* (see Appendix II, rule 3a).
There are two common patterns which it is particularly useful
to recognise: (a) a word of three long syllables with the
stress-pattern: ! ! ! = ictus-accent-ictus e.g. *transmittunt*;
and (b) a word of four syllables, having the pattern: ! / !
= ictus-accent-unstressed-ictus e.g. *interea*.

2. *The End of the Line* (see Appendix II, Rule 2). The
normal hexameter line (see note 21 for exceptions) ends with a
'double cadence', formed by the coincidence of the last two
ictuses and the last two accents. This is often extended to

coincidence of the last three ictuses and accents, giving a
'triple cadence'. In order to recognise the point at which
the cadence, double or triple, begins, it is useful to
remember that, once we have reached the caesura, there are
just two possibilities,

(a)   the next ictus after the caesura coincides with an
accent, and the cadence begins here - a triple cadence after
a third ictus caesura, a double cadence after a fourth, e.g.:

*ecce ferae saxi : deiectae uertice caprae* (triple cadence
after third ictus caesura);

*tecta metu petiere;  ruunt : de montibus amnes* (double cadence
after fourth ictus caesura).

*or*

(b)   a third ictus caesura is followed by an ictus not
coinciding with an accent, and the double cadence then begins
on the next stressed syllable (see Appendix II, Rule 3b), e.g.:

*decurrere iugis; : alia de parte patentis*

Type (b) is commoner than either of the two types (a).


*From Marked Text to Reading at Sight*

It now remains only to read through the text we have just
marked repeatedly, until it is secure enough to turn back to
its first appearance under the previous heading, and to find
in the plain text both the counterpoint of ictus and accent,
and also the phrasing.

Next, the procedure set out under the previous heading can
serve as a model for marking a copy of any chosen passage,
and practising it to the point where you can dispense
with the marked copy and still experience a full reading from
the plain printed text.

Finally, we are ready to dispense with markings altogher,
and to follow some such procedure as that here suggested
*in our minds* as we read.  When that begins to happen, we
are approximating to reading the text as Vergil and his
friends must have read it.

# PART VIII: SOUND AND SENSE

We hear much of the 'music' of Vergil's poetry. The
word comprises everything that does not come from the actual
meanings of the individual words and the word-structure
that he uses. It includes the rhythm of the metre and its
interaction with word-accent, as well as the phrasing and
the impact of the actual sounds, the resonance set up by
the repetition or echoing of sounds and sound-patterns.

A great deal of study has been devoted to the role of sound
in Latin poetry (see especially L.P. Wilkinson's *Golden Latin
Artistry*), and this is no place to make any kind of attempt
to do justice to the subject. In fact, strictly speaking,
there is no need to say anything about sound-patterns in a
guide to reading. Provided the sounds are actually made,
the patterns (if they are real) will simply be there in
what is heard. But as with some other things, so here the
ability to hear depends partly on knowing what we are hearing: it is in part a matter of trained awareness.

We know that Latin verse, before it came under Greek influ-
ence, was founded on stress and on assonance, rather like
Old English or Welsh verse. This assonance is more than
the significant repetition of single sounds, which is alliteration. Assonance involves the repetition of groups
of sounds, of which end-rhyme as we know it in English is
just one very specialised form. Rhyme is not important in
Classical Latin verse; assonance permeates it, changing
from a controlling principle in pre-Classical verse, through
an often bold and obvious use of it by earlier Classical
poets, to the subtle and sophisticated enrichment of the
verse that we find in Vergil or Horace.

It does, therefore, seem worthwhile to try to outline the
range and function of assonance in Vergil. And here a word
of caution. We shall be operating with the concept of
'significant repetition', by which we mean the echoing of a
sound (alliteration), or a group of sounds (assonance),
in a way that really does impinge on our ears - or would do
so on those of the practised reader - and did do so in the
poet's composing mind. Not to miss what is there, and not
to import what is not there; to sense when the recurrence
of sounds is to be registered at some level of awareness,
and when sounds are not connecting with other sounds in
this way, is always a matter of judgment and approximation.

Despite Tennyson's complaint that he often had no end of
trouble to get rid of alliteration, yet it seems clear that
*some* of the assonance that comes into a poet's composing
mind is welcome; indeed some of it is sought out and con-

49

sciously manipulated. More often, perhaps, it is a question
of those spontaneous processes of association which are
at work in the subliminal levels of poetic composition.
Underlying the choice and combination of words out of which
the conscious mind composes the text there are subtle
interacting processes at work all the time. One of these
is surely sound-association. And here we encounter a highly interesting observation. In strongly inflected languages
like Latin it would be easy for there to be a good deal of
assonance, especially assonance linking two words to each
other, simply through the recurrence of the same endings.
But in fact Vergil seems to be at some pains to avoid this
effect in his choice of words and constructions. Thus in
the specimen text, out of 27 instances of noun-adjective
combinations, only five have identical endings, four of
them being the short final *a* of the neuter nominative and
accusative plural;while the *ferae ... deiectae ... caprae*
of line 2 has no parallel elsewhere in these 22 lines.
This phenomenon bears a kind of negative witness to Vergil's
sensitivity to significant assonance of a subtler kind,
which would hardly have registered against the mechanical
and dominant effect of recurring case-endings. It also
explains why end-rhyme was so long resisted: if it has its
dangers in a language like our own, how much more in a
suffix-dominated language like Latin will it lay a heavy
hand on the sound-play of the poetry?

We will now therefore look at four types of significant
sound-recurrence or sound-patterns,namely: simple resonance;
word-linking; specific sound enhancement of the sense (ono-
matopoea); and unspecific sound-enhancement of the sense. We
should note that Latin spelling is in general a good guide
for our purposes, since on the whole the same letter always
represents the same sound. However, there are inevitable
exceptions and refinements (e.g. nasal *g* before *n*; final *m*);
and, in particular, the letters *a e i o* and *u* each represent
a long and a short vowel; and with the exception
of *a*, the long vowel is not simply a prolonged speaking
of the short one, but also slightly more closed. In
repeating a group of letters, therefore, long and short
vowels are akin but not identical; it seems that there is
still a real, if weaker, potential assonance between long
and short, helped no doubt by their visual identity.


*Simple Resonance*

The repetition of a cluster of sounds - two sounds recurring
at least three times, three or more sounds recurring at least
twice, *whether in the same order or not* - may set up a
resonance, a ringing quality, which simply enriches the
sound of what is being said, rather like an echo-chamber,
without contributing anything further to the meaning of what
is being said. In lines 20-22 of the specimen text, for

example, we have:

*... nEQue enim spECie faMaVE MoVETUR,*
*nEC iam fURTiuum Dido meditaTUR amorem:*
*COniugium uOCat, hOC praetECsit nominE Culpam.*

We might hear significant assonance of more than one sound-
group throughout these three lines, or just in line 22, or
not at all.  What we do not need is any specific evidence
that Vergil actually sought this effect; only that he
would have heard, and enjoyed, the faintly ringing echo
of  these repeating sounds (assuming that they do not
have any further function of a semantic kind, i.e. that
they do not help to convey something of his meaning).

Sometimes the repetition of a sound-cluster has almost the
character of an anagram: in the specimen text we have *PArTE
PATEntis* (line 3) as an interrupted repetition; *pecorA INTER
INERTIA* (line 8) and *SIGNum ... IGNeS* (line 17) as re-
shuffled groups.

An interesting question arises over the *interea* of line 10,
which repeats the *INTER INERTIA* grouping of line 8, but after
a major break (and is linked, perhaps, to the repeating
IN/NI sounds in lines 10f: *INterea magno ... INcipit, IN-
sequitur commixta grandINe NImbus*).  Is the resonance of
*INTEREA* purely fortuitous, or may the resonance in fact have
worked like an unconscious association in the poet's composing mind, suggesting the word *interea* from among several
that might have begun the new section for him?

If it is a matter of judgment whether there is a significant
resonance present or not, it is even more a matter of
judgment whether a given recurring sound-pattern is doing
anything more than just resonating.  It seems useful to
establish first of all that sometimes there is nothing more
involved than a sheer enrichment of sound, as being something pleasurable in itself, provided it remains unobtrusive.


*Word-linking*

Sometimes a resonance seems to acquire a semantic significance,
to contribute something to the meaning, when it links two or
more words to each other by their sound.  A good illustration
of this effect is provided by the words *Dido dux* in line 15
of the specimen text, which readers have sometimes been
misled into taking in grammatical agreement with each other
by the alliteration, whereas of course *dux* actually goes with
*Troianus*.  In line 22, over and above the resonances already
noted, the alliteration of *C* may help to bind in powerful
contrast the first and last words of the line *Coniugium ...
Culpam*.  Other instances from our text where resonance
may function in this way include the following:

CONscius aetherCONubiis (lines 17f.), and mONtE leONem
(line 9), both of which contain a particular effect,
that of a sequence of vowels being repeated or reversed.
A further powerful instance of this is aliA dE PArTE
PATEntis (line 3) which links together the words which
are turning our attention away from the slopes and peaks
to the 'openness in the other direction' towards the
plains.

Obviously, the effect described here is entailed in any
repetition of the same word, as in line 19: PRIMUS leti
PRIMUSque malorum (an effect which is further heightened
when the ictus-accent pattern is identical, as it is not
here). Vergil shows none of the need we feel to avoid
using the same word apparently unintentionally in fairly
close proximity, e.g. cursu (lines 4 and 7), preceded by
decurrere in line 3; we should, however, note the
contrast between e.g. campos and agros (lines 4 and 13),
and fuga and metu (lines 5 and 14) in two very similar
descriptions. But there is one repeated sequence that
stands out: MONTIS ... MONTISque ... MONTE ... MONTIBUS
(lines 1, 5, 9 and 14). This repetition of a key word
in four key lines (all of them the first or last lines
of sub-sections) is a masterstroke of subliminal suggestion,
keeping those mountains before our imagination.

## Specific Sound-enhancement of the Sense (Onomatopoea)

Sometimes an individual word actually suggests its own
meaning by its sound, and is no doubt chosen for that
reason. We actually hear the wailing or hallooing of the
nymphs in ULULarunt in line 18. A more extended instance
is afforded by the clicking and clattering of the jumping
goats in line 2:

ECCE ferae sACsi deiECTae uerTICE CAprae

So too in line 10 we have the ominous gathering of the storm:
Magno Misceri MURMURe, where repeated m's suggest power, as
they often do (cf. for instance Aeneid 4.449: Mens iMMota
Manet). And, of course, MURMURe rumbles powerfully in our
ears. Yet here we already begin to shade off into the
situation where a sound-pattern does not have a specific
quality of meaning in itself: after all, murmur can mean
'murmur' as well as 'rumble', so the sound MUR cannot be
threatening in itself.

## Unspecific Sound-enhancement of the Sense

And so we come to the most fascinating of the significant
uses of sound: a resonance is set up which has no specific

quality of its own, but which contributes something else
over and above the sheer enrichment of sound, the 'echo-
chamber' effect.  What happens here is that the echoing
of sound-groups co-operates with the meanings of the words
and word-groups in which the sounds occur, as well as with
their rhythm, their position and their phrasing, in such a way
as to acquire the colouring of its context: the sound-pattern
becomes like a mirror in which the quality of that context
is reflected and thereby enhanced.

Obviously we begin with the repetition of a key word, such
as that of *MONT-* as we have already noted it above.  We
have also already looked at *Alia dE PARTE PATEntis*, noting
the heavy assonance between *parte* and *patentis*.  To this we
must now add, first the vowel-sequence *A-E*, enhanced by the
following word *TRAnsmittunt*, which stands out in contrast
to the marked *E-I-U* sequence of what precedes; and second, the
linking of *PARTE* and *PATEntis* is carried on by *TRAns-*, and
the sequence of *A*'s has a potential for sounding 'open'
here precisely because of the attention focussed on the
word *patentis* in its strong position at the line-end and,
therefore, before a minor pause.  The openness of the plains
across which we are to watch the stampede of antelope is
precisely the thing that Vergil wants us to picture in
contrast to the rocky ridges on which we have just seen
(and heard) the leaping goats.  When we find another remarkable series of *A*'s in line 6, we will not for one moment experience it as conveying a quality of 'openness',
for the line is set 'deep in the glens':

*At puer AscAnius mediis in uAllibus Acri*

Rather, we may feel it conveys a sense of eagerness and
determination which becomes explicit in *acri*.

In line 8 the words *pecora* and *inertia* are surely Ascanius'
own contemptuous words for the goats and antelope - we are
inside his mind at this moment, and the assonance of *inter
inertia* may catch *his* intensity of feeling here.

Again, in line 9, the effect of vowel-sequence we have already
noted in *mONtE lEONem* must now be combined, first, with the
effect of the double coincidence on the *O*'s (short and long
though they be) and, above all, on the very strong position
of the phrase.

We have already noted how, in lines 10f., the sound of the
word *murmure* takes its colour from this specific context
and so enhances it.  We have also noted the resonance of
repeated *in*, which in fact begins both these closely-linked
lines and, in the second of those lines, further links the
two main verbs: *INterea ... INcipit, INsequitur*.  These
words contain a veritable barrage of *I*-sounds, *IncIpIt
InsequItur*, which co-operate with the juxtaposition of the

second main verb and the first to convey a sense of there
being no respite in the rapid descent of this freak storm.
As for *MISCeri* ... *coMMICSta* (supported by *inCIpit
inseQUItur*), the sound-echo may intensify the sense of chaos
conveyed by the meaning of the two words, though the effect
seems to be weakened by the fact that *MIS-* occurs at the
'low' point of the line.

It is interesting that both *pULuerULenta* in line 5 and
*DArDAniusque* in line 13 are homodyne dactylic words containing a repeating sound-group, as though this helps to speed
them along even faster, each in its respective stampede.
In line 14 it may be that the recurrence of syllables beginning with *T* co-operates with the dactyls and the very unusual
mid-line pause (one short syllable past the 3rd ictus) to
continue the stampeding effect: *TecTa mETu pETiere*; //.
(In fact the same sounds are already prominent in line 12:
*ET TYrii comiTEs passim-eT Troiana iuvEnTus*, though notably
absent from the intervening line 13.)

Lines 15-16 contain a repetition of *UN/NU* in *spelUNcam,
troiaNUs, deveniUNt proNUba* and *IUNo*; perhaps, however, it
is the echoing in *prONUBa IUNO* which makes a fateful link
to *cONUBiis* at the beginning of line 18. In the case of
*ULULarunt*, on the other hand, the preceding *speLUncam,
teLLUs* and *fULsere* seem at most to set up a possible resonance;
and certainly the preceding *pULVerULenta, FULVum* and *FULsere*
seem too far apart to do even that. Of course there remains the
potential for the use of one word to suggest another to the
poet in the way we have already discussed for the *interea*
of line 10: perhaps *puluerulenta/fuluum/fulsere* or *commixta/
comites* are possible instances of such non-significant
repetition.

The solemn force of the phrase *ILLE dIEs* (line 19) depends
in part on the repeated vowel-sequence, which is then
continued into *prImus LEtI*. There is strong assonance
between *MALORUM* and *AMOREM*, both at the line-end, but one
line apart: if it is significant, it is heavy with irony,
and that may not be in tune with the context. We have already noted extensive resonance in lines 20-22, and also
the significant alliteration of *Coniugium ... Culpam*. We
may now add that the sound-patterns, particularly in line 22,
seem to suggest the crisp clarity of Vergil's summing-up.

Finally, let us stress once more the importance of *non-
significance* of repeating sound. Immediately following our
specimen text, Vergil introduces his personification of
Rumour (*Aeneid* 4.173):

*Extemplo Libyae magnas it Fama per urbes,/ Fama ...*

Are we to sense significant recall of the *famaue* three lines
earlier, in line 20 of the specimen text? Surely not, for

it does not stand out there, in meaning, rhythm or position.
It may be a case of a word used in one piece of composition
suggesting itself for another in the poet's mind.   Or it may
be just coincidence.

*Conclusion*

In Vergil, sound-patterning is always a means, never an end
in itself; always subservient to, never dominant over the
primary elements of communication, namely, the meaning-
content of the words, singly and in groups, explicit and
implicit.   This is equally true of the other elements we have
been concerned with - the rhythm and its counterpoint with
word-accent, the interplay of metre and meaning in the phrasing.   Vergil may be the supreme master of verbal music,
but when Samuel Taylor Coleridge asks: 'Take away from
Vergil his metre and his diction, and what have you left?',
we have to reply: his meaning - and it is paramount.
Vergil is the  master of verbal music precisely because
that music is fulfilled in his meaning.

EPILOGUE


Ever since the 'reformed' pronunciation of Latin was
pioneered in this country a century or so ago, we have
aspired more and more to an 'authentic' experience of Latin
literature - to read it more nearly as if we were Romans
living in the great age of Cicero and Catullus, Vergil
and Horace. This aspiration covers the whole spectrum
from making the sounds they made to sharing the thought-
world in which they lived. And of course the aspiration
is unattainable. It is unattainable not just because
our knowledge and our understanding are and will remain
limited and uncertain: it is impossible for us existentially
to get inside their skin. Or rather - it may be possible
for us sometimes to have an informed empathy with those
who created this literature and those for whom they created
it. But we cannot know when and how far we are sharing the
authentic quality of their experience, for there is no
feedback to tell us so. And even insofar as we do enter
into their experience, we do so without for one moment
ceasing to be our own twentieth century, English-speaking
selves. We must accept that authentic reading of Latin
literature is impossible, just like translation - and that,
also like translation, it is the inevitable aspiration of
a living Classical tradition.

There is a great deal we would like to know about the way
in which its first readers read the *Aeneid* - aloud, of
course. First and foremost: what was their pace or tempo,
their speed of delivery? Next, what range of volume did
they use, and what range of pitch? A phonograph recording
of William Gladstone, made almost a century ago, makes
astonishing listening today, as his voice (then past its
prime) ascends and descends the musical scale like a solo
instrument, while varying rather less in volume around a
fairly strong mean. Again, how much emotional modulation
did they put into their voice, how much tonal versatility
in impersonation and mimicry did they allow themselves -
in a word, how many voices might one reader use?

Or we might put these questions in a different way, and ask:
what range and balance was there in their reading of the
*Aeneid* between different styles, all available and recognised:
oratory, as before an assembly on a public occasion; drama,
as in the theatre; the detached, objective tone of the
historian; or the intimacy of personal sharing in private
that belonged to lyric? Was there a standard 'epic' style
of reading, to which everyone would expect to approximate,
or was it largely an individual matter? We have a rather
general definition of reading from Vergil's contemporary
Varro, quoted by Diomedes, (*Gramm. Lat.*, ed. Keil, 1.426):

*lectio est artificialis interpretatio, uel uaria cuiusque*
*scripti enuntiatio seruiens dignitati personarum exprimens-*
*que animi habitum cuiusque.* 'Reading is the artificial
(artistic?) interpretation, or varied vocal presentation,
of each (kind of) writing, serving (to convey) the dignity
of the characters and expressing their individuality.'

Vergil, although he found continuous reading to others a
strain, had a very remarkable delivery (according to *Vita*
*Donati*, handily available in English as Appendix 1 of
W.A. Camps *An Introduction to Virgil's* Aeneid): Pronuntiabat
autem cum suauitate et cum lenociniis miris (*Vita* 27-8):
'His delivery had a sweetness and a wonderfully captivating
charm'. The *Vita* goes on to mention an obscure rival poet
who claimed that 'there were things he would steal from
Vergil, if he could (first) steal his voice, his facial
expression and his (talent for) acting'. That sounds like
something individual rather than stereotyped; something
expressive and modulated, but subtle rather than flamboyant.

As for us, each of us must develop our own style of reading,
within the constraints of our own *Zeitgeist*. A style like
Gladstone's, for instance, is not possible today, for it
would sound like a send-up of the text. Four recommendations
may be made: a moderate overall tempo, variation, elevation
and intimacy.


*A Moderate Overall Tempo*

In bare figures, ten hexameters or less to the minute, as
compared with twelve or more for Homer.

 There are good grounds for thinking that a moderate speed
of delivery is right for Latin, particularly Latin verse, as
compared with Greek, or with English. It has something to
do with the preponderance of long syllables, and the relative
economy of short, light words, which characterises Latin,
at least in the highly literary form in which we know it.
Moreover, we saw in Part VII that the theory of ictus-accent
interplay suggests that verse would have been read with an
artificially deliberate stressing which would naturally tend
to slow down delivery. Indeed, such a delivery seems necessary if ictus-accent counterpoint is actually to register in
our ears.

Not only the artistry of stress-patterns and of sound-patterns,
but also the impact of individual words depends on enough
time being allowed for the mind to register them. One of the
effects that is largely lost in translation is that produced
by the sheer duration of many a Latin word, and the weight
and stress-energy which this allows it to generate. 'To
war down the proud' is a striking phrase in English; faithful
and striking a translation though it is, it does not do justice

to débellāre supérbos, for if we give those two words their
full time, they conjure up the irresistible might of Rome.

Paradoxically, inexperience makes us rush - and makes it
harder for us to develop the very things that we may be
wanting, such as better habits of pronunciation, a sense
of rhythm and of counterpoint, a command of phrasing,
and an ear for resonance. And a leisurely tempo is also the
foundation for our remaining three recommendations.


*Variation*

This includes variation in the speed of delivery; in the length
of  pauses; in the range of volume and of pitch (within
the modest limits allowed by modern convention); in the use
of emphasis; in the tonality of the voice; and in the use of
various recognisable styles.

Variation expresses changes of mood and tone, and, together
with longer pauses, is the way in which the *ear* can organise
a text into manageable units.  The  eye knows by means of
full stops and other means that it is moving from one
section to the next; the ear only knows it through the voice.
It is natural for inexperience to 'play safe' in a rather
inexpressive monotony; for fear of sounding wrong, one finds
oneself making the poetry sound nondescript.  It may be
necessary at some stage to cultivate variation - almost any
variation - for its own sake: this will provide the raw
material on which discrimination and judgment can then begin
to work.

We have already become familiar with the idea of an interaction
between two complementary elements - ictus and accent in the
stressing, meaning and metre in the phrasing.  The two remaining headings deal with another such pair, this time at the
level of imaginative interpretation.  For in the *Aeneid* there
is a tension between two qualities which are opposite yet
inseparable.


*Elevation:* 'sua praemia laudi' (Aen. 1.461)

There is no doubt a sense in which the grand scale, and the
lofty conception, of the *Aeneid* invest every part of the poem
with epic dignity.  Indeed, in comparison with Homer, there is
a very Roman tendency towards the massive and monumental.
*Ingens* is one of Vergil's favourite words; and whereas Hector
easily manhandles a stone that two of the very best men could
hardly have lifted in Homer's day, by Vergil's time it would
have taken twelve of the best to carry the rock that Turnus
hurls with a single hand.  There may be times when authen-
ticity will actually go against the grain - though most modern
readings of the poem do also find Vergil himself deeply

ambivalent about the imperial dimension.

But far deeper than the imperial theme, and at the very heart
of his art, there is a sense that nothing in Vergil is casual;
that everything, great or small, is invested with a certain
value and status. Whether we like it or not - and we have
grown rather wary of conscious dignity - a sense of elevation
is there *all the time* in Vergil, and is meant to be there.
In the *Georgics*, as he is about to embark on the theme of
sheep and goats, he says (3.289-90): *nec sum animi dubius
uerbis ea uincere magnum / quam sit et angustis hunc addere
rebus honorem*, 'nor am I in any doubt in my own mind how great
a task it is to master these themes with words, and thus
dignify things that are lowly'. Lovers of Vergil have always
felt that his elevation rings true, at least most of the
time, because it celebrates an inherent dignity in things.
Yet paradoxically, if it does ring true, it does so especially
today precisely because it also has another face.

*Intimacy:* 'mentem mortalia tangunt' (Aen. 1.462)

We know that Vergil was a highly self-conscious artist.
According to the *Vita* (22), 'When he was writing the *Georgics*,
it is said that it was his custom to compose and dictate a very
large number of lines every morning, and to spend the rest of
the day re-working and reducing them to a very few, saying
rather aptly that he was like a she-bear giving birth to his
poem and then licking it into shape.' In fact, the *Georgics*
grew at the rate of one line a day; this speed was pushed up
to over two lines a day for the Aeneid. Out of such a work-
shop comes the conscious artistry of his poetry, and the sense
of a special intimacy with the fabric of his own writing.
No doubt this was also part of what people heard in his own
reading, to some aspects of which we have sought to gain
access in this booklet.

Alongside this quality of intimacy with the verbal fabric of
his text, there is in Vergil the sense of another kind of
intimacy - with the actual fabric of the world; or rather,
with the consciousness of that world. He does, of course,
enlist our powers of imagination, of visual representation,
as we look at the scenes that he sets before us. But it is
his special gift to look at the world *from within* the actors
in those scenes, capturing and heightening the mental experience of things, of events, of inner processes. The essence
of this power of empathy (which is something distinct from
sympathy, though often linked with it) is to engage with the
sentient world as it were from the inside, through an inward
and intimate sensibility. And the cues for this engagement
are given again and again through his use of language.

If we can hold a sense of intimacy in tension with a sense of
elevation, we have a key to release our best powers into our

reading of the *Aeneid*. Vergil found in that tension his
labour of love: *amor* drew him to every little theme that
he touched, *amor* drove him to its elevation into poetry
(*Georgics* 3.285, 292). So too, when all is said and done
about ways and means, it is *amor* that gives authentic life
to the reading of Vergil.

NOTES

1. For the underlying theory, see three books by W.S. Allen:
   *Vox Latina* (2nd edn. 1978),esp. p.126; *Vox Graeca* (2nd ed.1974),
   especially pp.120-4 and 161; *Accent and Rhythm* (1973). See
   also my 'On the Authentic Reading of Hexameter Poetry' in
   *Aufstieg und Niedergang der Romischen Welt II 35* (forthcoming), edd. Haase and Temporini.
       The idea that the rhythm of the hexameter arises from a
   sequence of six stresses, of the same kind as the stress of
   word-accent (dynamic accent), is now familiar enough for
   Latin. The idea that Greek has a subsidiary stress accent
   as well as its dominant tonal accent, and that this accent is
   the basis of rhythm in Greek also, will come as a surprise
   to many (see Appendix II in the parallel booklet *Homer's
   Metre*, Bristol Classical Press, 1986). See also note 3 below.

2. Other differences contribute to the same effect; for instance,
   the absence in Latin of a definite article, and the much
   reduced presence of short 'particles'.

3. See again note 1. The basic rule of the (subsidiary) stress
   accent in Greek is that it falls on the last long syllable
   of the word (with, of course, various refinements). This
   hypothesis gives 90-95% coincidence between ictus and accent
   in Homer's hexameter, whose rules would then be presumed
   to have arisen in response to the rules governing word-stress
   in Greek. But the rules governing word-stress in Latin are
   different, and there is therefore no longer the same re-
   sponsiveness when the hexameter pattern is transferred
   into this different linguistic medium. On the contrary,
   the rules of the hexameter, which did not develop out of
   the Latin stress system, now tend to ensure that there will
   *not* be uniform coincidence of ictus and accent, with the mid-
   line division in particular being made to militate against it
   in the first three or four feet of the line (the fourth foot
   of the Latin hexameter characteristically contains an ictus
   but no accent). See further note.22.

4. However, it should perhaps be admitted that to read the hexameter as prose with correct accentuation will still convey
   the movement of the metre through the cadence (where there is
   always coincidence between verse-beat and word-accent), and
   through other coincidences in most lines. The fact is that
   Latin hexameters, unlike Greek, can be read quite tolerably
   by someone ignorant of the metre - much more tolerably than
   by drumming out the metre in violation of the natural accentuation of many of the words. And yet - to read Vergil and
   ignore the hexameter seems unthinkable!

5. But see below for the virtually fixed pattern of the cadence,
   and note 7. Greek and Latin verse operates a 'principle of
   indifference', whereby the final syllable of any metre can

be either long or short (see W.S. Allen, *Accent and Rhythm*, s.v. 'indifference' in the index). We do not really know what to make of the phenomenon. As far as the hexameter is concerned, it means that the sixth foot can be either a spondee (--) or a trochee (-ᴗ).

It seems plausible, however, that in Greek the hexameter was felt to end in a 'catalectic' or stopping-short dactyl (*not* a trochee), whose final short syllable is replaced by, or perhaps absorbed into, the required minor pause at the line-end (see Part V). A normally long syllable could also stand in the final position, but was shortened, thereby preserving both the rhythm (by shifting the stress on the last long syllable of the word back on to the penultimate syllable, see note 3 above) and also the catalectic dactyl as well (see the companion booklet *Homer's Metre*, Appendix II).

But when this metre is adapted to Latin, the principle of indifference tends to operate in the opposite direction, by using more final short syllables to make the line end with a spondee, with the minor pause of the line-end now established in its own right. We therefore arrive at a convenient standardisation whereby we count the final syllable as always short in Greek and always long in Latin.

6. Greek and Latin verse is quantitative. This does not mean that it has no beat based on the difference between stressed and unstressed syllables, as we have in English verse. It means that in Greek and Latin, unlike English and other modern European languages, the verse-beat is something that arises out of a particular pattern of long and short syllables for each metre (for stress in Greek, see *Homer's Metre*, Appendix II). See also note 11.

7. A distinction is nowadays drawn between spoken metres and sung metres in Greek metrical theory. The former do not have feet and were never linked with dance; instead, they have 'measures' (Greek, *metron*). The musical analogy offered here is not meant to imply that the hexameter was sung but only to be a conceptual aid for understanding quantity - with perhaps an eye to that other possible origin in the rhythm-tapping foot.

8. In Latin the final syllable is always counted as long (see note 5). An alternative cadence, with a fifth foot spondee, is quite acceptable though not common in Greek. In Latin such a cadence is best regarded as a special stylistic effect, and in Vergil in particular an editor would draw attention to such a cadence in his notes.

9. See Appendix IV, and see Part V for the subtle presence of the caesura in live reading.

10. For the departure from traditional scansion, see the end of the Introduction, and Appendix V.

11. In modern theory only vowels are termed 'long' and 'short',
    while syllables are described as having 'heavy' or 'light'
    quantity.  But the habit of calling syllables long and short,
    though potentially confusing (see next note), is ingrained
    from Ancient times; and it remains true that duration is
    *one* element - perhaps, after all, the decisive element as
    the Ancients themselves thought - in the difference between
    two kinds of syllable.  See also the Preface.

12. The symbol - can therefore stand not only over a long vowel,
    but also over a short vowel in a long (strictly heavy)
    syllable.  Such a vowel remains short, that is, its pronun-
    ciation does not change because it stands in a long syllable
    and is marked long: the - in this case shows that the syl-
    lable counts as long in the metre, and this is what we are
    primarily concerned with.

13. At the line-end, with its required minor pause or suspension
    (see Part V), such a gap is necessary and natural, and the
    rule for vowel-junction does not apply - as for instance bet-
    ween lines 1 and 2, or 10 and 11, of the specimen text.  Those
    rare exceptions in which a 'hypermetric' line does indeed
    end with an elided vowel will always be pointed out by an
    editor in his notes.
       Occasionally, and in Vergil always for deliberate effect,
    the metre requires *both* vowels to be fully retained at a
    vowel-junction: there is a *hiatus*, which again editors normal-
    ly point out in their notes.  A good example is *Eclogues*
    8.41:

    ut *uidi*, -ut *perii*, ut me malus abstulit error!

    'Even as I saw (you), so I was lost, so an evil delusion stole
     me away',

    where the hiatus between *perii* and *ut*, which must both be pro-
    nounced in full to fill the metre, helps to suggest a break
    or sob in the speaker's voice.

14. The Latin hexameter requires a strong caesura, i.e. one
    immediately following an ictus; whereas the Greek hexameter
    equally admits a weak caesura following the first short after
    the third ictus.  This gives a 'falling' movement in mid-line
    much like that of the cadence at the line-end; it seems to
    suit the lighter, more rapid but less intense movement of
    the Greek as against the Latin metre (see also Introduction
    and note 2).
       Moreover, it is clear that the elimination of the weak
    caesura tends, in Latin, to ensure that the first three or
    four ictuses will not all coincide with the natural word-
    accents, as do the fifth and sixth - so producing that inter-
    play of ictus and accent which gives the Latin hexameter its
    own, quite different, flexibility from that of the Greek
    metre with its more mobile caesura.
       The Greek weak caesura is occasionally used in Latin - by
    Vergil always for special effect.  So at *Aeneid* 2.9, 4.486,

and 5.856, it is used to suggest soothing, irresistable
sleepiness, with two of the lines having total coincidence
of ictus and accent (and two also using very powerful
assonance).

15. But a preposition is felt to 'lean' so closely onto the
next word that no caesura can, as it were, get between them.
So in line 1 of the specimen text, the caesura would come
after *montis* and the fourth ictus, not after *in* and the
third ictus. The same can also apply to conjunctions; so
with *et ... et* in line 16, the caesura would come after
*tellus* and the fourth ictus, not after the third ictus on
the first *et*. But otherwise the rule should be applied
strictly, with the caesura coming after the third ictus
regardless of the phrasing of the sense.

16. We shall not be concerned here with that level in the linking
or grouping of words by grammar and position which is too
fine to be registered by the voice or by the ear, and which
belongs rather to a particular way of analyzing the structure
of language.

17. The next most common pauses occur before the second ictus
and before the fifth ictus; this latter, called the 'bucolic
diaeresis' because it is very common in bucolic, or pastoral,
verse like Vergil's *Eclogues*, is not found in our specimen
text here. (For the distinction between caesura and diaeresis,
see the beginning of Appendix IV.)  S.E. Winbolt *Latin
Hexameter Verse* (1903), repr. 1983), ch.1, contains a fascinating review of pauses, especially as used by Vergil.

18. Clearly, in the mind of the composing poet, the phrasing must
be a function of the flow of the sense over several lines,
and the reader can only approximate to this state of mind in a
second reading. While a reader must be able to follow the
basic rhythm of the metre at sight (see the conclusion of
Appendix IV), sensitive interpretation, including the finer
phrasing, operates at a different level, and will require
study, or at least improve with study.

19. It has become usual in discussions of Latin poetry to use the
terms 'coincidence' and 'conflict' for what is here being
described. But 'conflict' is a loaded word, whereas 'alternation' is neutral, like coincidence, leaving open what impression the interaction may convey in any given case (see also
note 23 below). Another set of terms in use is 'homodyne'
and 'heterodyne', i.e. coincidence and alternation respectively: see Appendix II.
     We should note that when we speak here of 'two different
kinds of stress' we are not talking about the voice being used
in two different ways, as between stress accent and pitch
accent, but about one and the same thing, namely, dynamic
accent or stress, arising in poetry in two different ways
simultaneously from the word-accent and from the verse-beat.

See the analogy of two 'waves' passing along a chain of
syllables, used below.

20. See the analysis of the specimen text in Appendix II. The
    recognition that the hexameter contains a regular number of
    word-accents as well as a fixed number of ictuses, is recent.
    L.P. Wilkinson makes interesting use of it in the note to his
    translation of Vergil's *Georgics* (Penguin 1982, p.55), where
    he commends the traditional 5-beat line of English blank
    verse, varied with an occasional 6-beat line in the manner
    of Dryden's translation, to carry Vergil into English.
    Even after C.Day Lewis, the 6-beat line with variable
    'troughs', based on the pattern of the hexameter itself,
    still feels strained and alien to many readers. In the
    case of Homer, where verse-beat and word-accent are almost
    identical (see note 3), there is no parallel case for a
    5-beat line; and it is interesting that Richmond Lattimore's
    line of 6 beats with variable 'troughs' seems to many more
    acceptable for the *Iliad* and *Odyssey* than does Lewis' for the
    *Aeneid*. Perhaps the reading of Vergil needs a certain sense
    of energy contained under tension within a formal discipline,
    which arises for us more readily from our traditional blank
    verse-form; whereas for Homer a sense of energy released in
    controlled but untrammelled flow makes the freer 6-beat
    line more acceptable.

21. Every departure from this pattern in Vergil seems designed
    for deliberate effect. There is no example in the specimen
    text, but a good one is the line adapted from Ennius at
    *Aeneid* 6.846:

    *unus qui nobis cunctando restituis rem*

    '(you) who alone by delaying restore our state',
    with its strong and stark final monosyllable.

22. When the foot preceding the cadence (double or triple) con-
    tains a monosyllable or pyrrhic, it *may* contain a word-accent.
    In the specimen text we have the following instances: elided
    *atque* (equivalent to a monosyllable) in lines 1 and 4; *de*
    in lines 3 and 14; *in* in line 6; *iam* in line 7; *et* in lines
    16 and 17; *hoc* in line 22, before a triple cadence. Of these,
    only the last and *iam* in line 7 might be stressed (see the
    analysis of the passage in Appendix II).
        Failure to appreciate that many, perhaps most, monosyllables
    and pyrrhics are unstressed has led to the impression that
    Vergil favoured alternation before the cadence, i.e. a
    heterodyne fourth foot, in contrast to his predecessors.
    The real change he made here was to make less use of the
    triple cadence, leaving the fourth foot typically as a low
    point or lull containing an ictus but no accent.

23. We recall that the metre itself has a 'rising' movement in
    the first half and a 'falling' movement in the second,
    divided at the caesura. The fact that the counterpoint of
    ictus and accent typically extends the first part beyond the

caesura would mean that the tension characteristic of the
first part of the line does not begin to resolve until
the metre is already well launched into its 'descent':
like so much else in this poetry, such an effect has a strong
aesthetic or psychological sense of rightness about it.
Incidentally, the word 'tension', with its Latin root meaning of 'stretching', hopefully does not suffer from the same
objection as the word 'conflict' (see note 19 above).

24. This effect arises from a combination of three factors: the
sheer weight of the three long ('heavy') syllables, their
slow movement, and their sustained energy.

## APPENDIX I: SOME OTHER METRES

### A   The Pentameter: Elegiac Couplets

The pentameter might be called the hexameter's shadow, for
it looks rather like it and never appears without it.   A
hexameter followed by a pentameter forms the so-called
elegiac couplet.   The full name 'dactylic pentameter'
(corresponding to the 'dactylic hexameter') declares that
the line consists of five 'measures' (Greek, *pente* and *metron*)
with a dactylic rhythm.   However, this count of five arises
in a curious way, giving the pentameter *six* ictuses - the
same number as the hexameter, but differently arranged.

The pentameter falls into two distinct halves, divided
precisely at the mid-point of the line.   The first
half is variable, consisting of two feet which may be
either dactyls or spondees, but ending invariably in a
single stressed long just before the break: ⏑ ⏑ ⏑ ⏑ ⏑.
This is two and a half measures, but three ictuses.   The
second half of the line is fixed, consisting of two dactyls
and a final stressed long syllable (see note 5 ): ⏑ ⏑ ⏑ ⏑ ⏑.
This is also two and a half measures, but three ictuses.   There
are therefore five measures or feet, but six ictuses.

There is a sense of the line first rising, then falling,
but with a precise balance at its mid-point quite unlike
the hexameter's.   Also different is the sense of finality
at the line-end, which tends to make the elegiac couplet
into a self-contained unit, ending in a major or at least a
minor sense-pause.   So Catullus introduces the soldier with
his extra *h*'s (84.1f.):

*Chommoda dicebat, : si quando commoda uellet /*
*  dicere,— et insidias : Arrius hinsidias. //*

If the hexameter is also end-stopped, the couplet acquires an
additional sense of neat internal balance.   So in one famous
couplet which constitutes a whole poem, Catullus states his
own inner conflict in the hexameter, and imagines someone
asking him to explain the reason for it; then, in the pentameter he gives his answer (85):

*Odi-et amo. // quare-id : faciam, fortasse requiris.//*
*  nescio, // sed fieri : sentio—et excrucior.//*

Like the hexameter, the pentameter shows more alternation
than coincidence of ictus and accent in its first half, more
coincidence than alternation in its second.   But in contrast
to the hexameter, the pentameter avoids the coincidence at
the line-end which produces a cadence.   In lines such as

those just quoted, alternation extends over the last four
syllables of the pentameter, embracing one that is unstressed: that at least seems to be the feeling, arising no doubt
from the effect of the following line-end pause. Increas-
ingly as time went by the pentameter was made to end with
a disyllable,

*in uento-et rapida : scribere-oportet aqua.* // (70.4).

Here the effect is to rein in the momentum generated by two
preceding coincidences: in combination with the frequent
major pause that follows, this is a very strong effect
which, if overdone, easily becomes rather stereotyped - so
that it is doubtful whether this tendency was really an
improvement on Catullus' more flexible practice. Altogether,
the pentameter has a sense of developing considerable energy
and then checking it more or less abruptly in its flow, giving it a very distinctive quality - crisp, firm, incisive,
brilliant.


B  Horace's Lyric Metres

Horace published four books of *Carmina* or 'Odes' and the
*Carmen Saeculare* in lyric metres: 104 pieces in all. Of
these most are written in four-line stanzas; in fact, even
those that do not demand to be read this way probably should
be.  The commonest metre is the Alcaic, named after the early
Greek lyric poet, Alcaeus of Lesbos: it accounts for about
one third of all the Odes.  Next comes the Sapphic stanza,
named after Alcaeus' contemporary and compatriot, the poetess
Sappho, used in about one quarter of the Odes.  Thirdly, a
further quarter of the total uses a group of related metres
called Asclepiads or 'Asclepiad systems' (after an obscure
late Greek poet who had revived the old Greek lyric metres
from the days of Sappho and Alcaeus).  Between them, these
three types account for five-sixths of all the Odes.

At first sight, the learning of all these metres might seem a
formidable task in comparison with the single metre needed to
read the whole of Vergil.  In fact, the hexameter is much
more difficult to read than are these lyric metres.  The main
reason for this is that the pattern of each lyric line is
totally, or almost totally, fixed and unvarying - whereas the
hexameter, of course, is subject to constant variation in
its first four feet.  The lyric lines are also much shorter,
and there are fewer vowel-junctions to cope with.  Once you
have understood one example of each type, every other will
fit neatly into the pattern.  Like all Latin verse, Horace's
lyric metres are scanned as sequences of long and short
syllables; but the crucial factor in their rhythm is the
verse-beat or ictus: since, in these lyric metres, the
ictus always falls in the same place (as it does not, of
course, in the hexameter), there is no need to decide whether

a syllable is long or short.  All we need for the *rhythm*
is to know which syllables in each line are stressed.

*Note.*  Of course the appreciation of syllable quantity - of long and
short - is an important element in the poetry too; something of this
will be seen in the  discussion of *General Characteristics*
below.  On the other hand, there no longer seems to be any question
nowadays of dividing Horace's lyric metres into feet; if at all, they
are analysed into longer units called cola (Greek, *kolon* = a limb).
Some editors, however, having dispensed with feet, give no indication
of the verse-beat, leaving the lines to stand as a rhythmically mean-
ingless sequence of longs and shorts.  For a full presentation see
D.S. Raven's *Latin Metre* (Faber, 1965), though it should be said that
my own presentation here is not directly based on Raven's nor wholly
in line with his.

We will now take each type in turn, marking the rhythm
both on a model text and on the sequence of long and short
syllables (for final syllables all counting as long, see
note 5):


*The Sapphic Stanza*

This stanza consists of a line of eleven syllables (called
the Sapphic Hendecasyllable or Lesser Sapphic) which is
thrice repeated, and then followed by a little rounding-off
line of five syllables (called the Adonic), e.g. 1.22.1-4:

*Integer uitae ⋮ scelerisque purus*

*non eget Mauris ⋮ iaculis neque-arcu*

*nec uenenatis ⋮ grauida sagittis,*

    *Fusce, pharetra,*

Occasionally the Sapphic line breaks one syllable later, after
six syllables rather than after five, e.g. 1.10.1:

*Mercuri, facunde ⋮ nepos Atlantis*


*The Asclepiad Systems*

Under this heading are grouped five related patterns, conventionally numbered from one to five and called the 'First
Asclepiad System', the 'Second Asclepiad System', and so
on (unfortunately not with universal consistency; the number-
ing adopted here is found in more recent books).

Four different lines appear in these systems in various
combinations: what they all have in common is the basic
rhythm: ⌐◡◡⌐, called a 'choriamb'.  Each of the four lines

used is an extension or expansion of this basic rhythmic
unit, which is picked out here by being underlined where-
ever it occurs. Here, first, is a schematic representation,
in terms of long or short syllables, of the relationship of
these four patterns to one another and to the basic
choriambic rhythm from which they all derive:

Choriamb

Glyconic

Pherecratean

Lesser Asclepiad

Greater Asclepiad

*Note*: the Pherecratean is obtained by removing the short syllable
separating the two stressed longs at the end of the Glyconic, giving
it a curious syncopated rhythm, rather like that of Catullus' 'limping
iambic'.


*First Asclepiad System*

This consists simply of a sequence of Lesser Asclepiad lines,
e.g. 3.30.1-5:

*Exegi monumentum- : aere perennius*

*regalique situ : pyramidum-altius,*

*quod non imber edax, : non Aquilo-impotens*

*possit diruere-aut : innumerablilis*

*annorum series : et fuga temporum.*


*Second Asclepiad System*

This consists of an alternation of Glyconics with Lesser
Asclepiads, i.e. of couplets which can and probably should be
grouped into four-line stanzas, e.g. 3.9.1-4:

*Donec gratus eram tibi*

*nec quisquam potior : bracchia candidae*

*ceruici iuuenis dabat,*

*Persarum uigui : rege beatior*

*Third Asclepiad System*

This is a true stanza, consisting of three Lesser Asclepiads
rounded off by a Glyconic, e.g. 1.24.1-4:

Quis desiderio ⋮ sit pudor aut modus     — — — ᴗᴗ — ⋮ — ᴗᴗ — ᴗ —

tam cari capitis? ⋮ praecipe lugubris     — — — ᴗᴗ — ⋮ — ᴗᴗ — ᴗ —

cantus, Melpomene, ⋮ cui liquidam pater     — — — ᴗᴗ — ⋮ — ᴗᴗ — ᴗ —

    uocem cum cithara dedit.     — — — ᴗᴗ — ᴗ —

*Fourth Asclepiad System*

Again a true stanza, and the most complex, consisting of two
Lesser Asclepiads, then a Pherecratean as line three, and a
Glyconic to close, e.g. 1.5.1-4:

Quis multa gracilis ⋮ te puer in rosa     — — — ᴗᴗ — ⋮ — ᴗᴗ — ᴗ —

perfusus liquidis ⋮ urget odoribus     — — — ᴗᴗ — ⋮ — ᴗᴗ — ᴗ —

    grato, Pyrrha, sub antro?     — — — ᴗᴗ — —

     cui flauam religas comam,     — — — ᴗᴗ — ᴗ —

*Fifth Asclepiad System*

Like the First, this system is simply a sequence of repeated
lines, this time of the Greater Asclepiad, e.g. 1.11.1:

Tu ne quaesieris, ⋮ scire nefas, ⋮ quem mihi, quem tibi

— — — ᴗᴗ — ⋮ — ᴗᴗ — ⋮ — ᴗᴗ — ᴗ —

*The Alcaic Stanza*

We now come to Horace's masterpiece. It uses three different
types of line, of which the first, with eleven syllables, is
sometimes called the Alcaic Hendecasyllable. This line is
repeated, forming lines one and two of the stanza. Line
three has nine syllables, line four has ten. The crucial
requirement, here as always, is to register which syllables
are stressed - and to note carefully that in lines 1, 2
and 3 the first stress comes on the *second* syllable, whereas
in line 4 it comes in the usual place, on the first syllable.
(The resulting unstressed first syllable of lines 1, 2 and 3
is called an 'anacrusis', a Greek word meaning a 'striking
up'.) Notice also that the eleven-syllable sequence, which forms
lines 1 and 2, is divided, whereas the other two are continuous, e.g. 1.37.1-4:

*Nunc est bibendum,* ⋮ *nunc pede libero*      --⌣-- ⋮ -⌣⌣-⌣-

*pulsanda tellus,* ⋮ *nunc Saliaribus*      --⌣-- ⋮ -⌣⌣-⌣-

*ornare puluinar deorum*      --⌣--⌣--

    *tempus erat dapibus, sodales.*      -⌣⌣-⌣⌣-⌣--

*General Characteristics*

The three types of rhythm set out above - the Sapphic,
Asclepiad and Alcaic - each have thier own distinctive individuality in terms of their overall quality or 'feel'.

*The Sapphic line* generates a good deal of power in its first
half, with its heavy syllables and its three stresses, but then
releases much of it in its rapid, falling or descending, second
half. This happens three times, until the stanza is rounded
off, as it were, by the little Adonic (which actually began
life as an extension tacked on to the  end of the Sapphic
line). Of course Horace occasionally makes his sense run on
over the end of a Sapphic stanza (as at 3.8.4), but not
very often: it seems to be hard for that Adonic not to bring
the run of three identical Sapphics to a clear, neat stop.

*The Asclepiad rhythms* are characterised by equilibrium. With
its eight, twelve or sixteen syllables, each line seems bal-
anced symmetrically about its own centre, with only a slight
sense of rise and fall within the line. The couplets of the
Second System flow smoothly by. In the Third System, the
final Glyconic after the three identical Lesser Asclepiads
has a rounding-off quality rather like that of the Adonic,
and the whole stanza has a feel as of a rather staid version
of the Sapphic. In the Fourth System we have the Pherecratean, with its odd number of seven syllables and curious
final syncopation: it produces a kind of over-balancing
effect in the third line which the closing Glyconic then
sets right again, making for a very attractive, almost play-
ful rhythm.

Horace's *Alcaic stanza* builds up a powerful rising or
ascending rhythm which does not reach its summit until the
third line. It arises partly from the effect of the
'anacrusis' of the first three lines, also from the greater
power generated in the second half of lines 1 and 2. Right
into line 3, then, there is a sense of pressing on or
gathering height. In line 3, with its symmetrical pattern,
there is a sense of levelling out - before the stanza plunges
steeply down, in its light and rapid fourth line, uninterrupted
for ten syllables. Like the others, the Alcaic is very ver-
satile in Horace's hands, but for sheer power and even a
touch of majesty it is unrivalled among his metres, and
sometimes even allows him to use two stanzas, as it were, as

a single block out of which to build a lofty poem (such as
3.1 or 3.29).  So much may be said of the general characteristics of Horace's lyric verse in terms of its metrical
patterns alone, but clearly it would also be much affected
by any interplay of ictus and accent, for which see Appendix IIB.


## C  Catullus' Metres

Catullus, or his editor, arranged his poems in such a way
that all those numbered 65 and upwards are in elegiacs
(see Appendix IA, above).  Nos. 61-4 are long poems,
mainly using either hexameters or a combination of Glyconics and Pherecrateans (see Appendix IB, above).

This leaves nos. 1-60: these are conventionally referred to
as the 'polymetric' poems, because they use many metres.
However, only two are really common: one is the so-called
'limping' iambic; the other is his favourite line, the
Phalaecian Hendecasyllable (Greek, *hendeka* = eleven), usually
just called the Hendecasyllable.  It is a continuous line without an obligatory mid-line break (and so the longest unbroken
unit in Latin poetry), and with a fixed rhythm except for
some variation permitted in its first two syllables, thus:

$$\text{---}\cup\cup\text{-}\cup\text{-}\cup\text{--}$$

or

$$\text{-}\cup\text{-}\cup\cup\text{-}\cup\text{-}\cup\text{--}$$

or

$$\cup\text{--}\cup\cup\text{-}\cup\text{-}\cup\text{--}$$

For example, these are the first four lines of the first
poem:

> Cui dōnō lepidum nouum libellum
>
> ārida modo pumice-expolitum?
>
> Cornēlli, tibi: namque tu solēbas
>
> meas esse-aliquid putare nugas.

The 'limping', or perhaps better 'skipping', effect produced
in the last line above by the two adjacent ictuses near the
beginning is the distinguishing feature from which the 'limping' iambic gets its name, but this time the effect is at
the end of the line (cf. Horace's Pherecratean, above).  The
line consists of five iambs ($\cup\text{-}$), with a final inverted stress
on a spondee ($\text{-}\text{-}$, see note 5).  Of the five iambs, the first
and third may also be spondees, but stressed on their second
syllable.  There is a caesura before the third ictus or,
failing that, before the fourth, e.g. 8.1,3:

*Míser Catúlle,* : *désinás inéptíre,*

*Fulsére quóndam* : *cándidí tibí sóles.*

The interplay of ictus and accent in Catullus is briefly
discussed at the end of Appendix II.

### Three Eleven-Syllable Lines

There are three lines of eleven syllables that are much
used in Latin lyric verse - two by Horace and one by Catullus.
Below are given examples of each of the three, and by means
of numbers the sequence of the *stressed* syllables in each
form is picked out.  The individuality of each of the three
rhythms arises from this sequence - and also from the fact
that Catullus' hendecasyllable has no regular point of internal division.  They are:

Horatian Sapphic Hendecasyllable (1.22.1):

*Intéger uítae* : *scelerísque púrus*   ${}^1 - {}^3\cup - - {}^5 - : \cup\cup {}^8 - {}^{10} -$

Horatian Alcaic Hendecasyllable (1.37.1):

*Nunc ést bibéndum,* : *nunc péde líberó*   $- {}^2 - \cup {}^4 - - : {}^6 - \cup\cup {}^9 - \cup {}^{11} -$

Catullus' Phalaecian Hendecasyllable (1.1-2):

*Cui dónó lépidúm nouúm libéllúm*   ${}^1 - {}^3 - - \cup\cup {}^6 - \cup {}^8 - \cup {}^{10} - -$

*árida módo púmice-expolítum?*   ${}^1 - {}^3 \cup - \cup\cup {}^6 - \cup {}^8 - \cup {}^{10} - -$

(*Note:* the Catullan form can begin $- -$ as in line 1, or $- \cup$ as
in line 2, or $\cup -$ as in line 4 of the same poem.)

The Rules of Interplay between Ictus and Accent in
the Hexameter


*Rule 1    The Number of Ictuses and Accents*

There are six ictuses, and normally five or six (occasionally
seven) accents.

*Note:*   If a line contains one or more words with an optional accent,
the number of accents in that line is to some extent a matter of
judgment (see below).  Only a line containing such a word can have
more than six accents.  The rule as here given for the number of
accents in a hexameter has arisen from the exercise of judgment over
a large number of words with an optional accent in Vergil (see also
note 20).  It is only fair to warn here that, once accepted, the rule
will tend to confirm itself, since it will become natural to exercise
the option in such a way as to observe the rule - which is precisely
what is recommended!

The concept of optional accent is applied to three types
of word: monosyllables; pyrrhics (two short syllables); other
disyllables ending in a vowel-junction; perhaps also tri-
brachs (three short syllables) ending in a vowel-junction.  To
treat the accent on all such words on all occasions as equally optional is a convenient simplification, since it covers
both those cases where an accent is clearly right or wrong,
and those where it is a question of discerning a preference
in the text.  For example, in lines 6-7 of the specimen text
(see also analysis below) we have: *in*: surely unaccented;
*puer*: most probably accented; *at*: probably unaccented; and
*iamque-hos ... iam*: surely one accented, but not all three,
so either one or two.  Any guidelines that might be offered
would be either so detailed, or so incomplete, as to be self-
defeating.  The concept of the optional accent at least avoids
prescribing anything wrong, and is most serviceable in practice.


*Rule 2    The Cadence - Double and Triple*

(a)    The hexameter line *must* end with a double cadence, formed
       by the coincidence of the last two ictuses and the last
       two accents, and so occupying the last two feet of the
       line (for exceptions, see note 21).

(b)    The hexameter line *may* end with a triple cadence, formed
       by the coincidence of the last three ictuses and the last
       three accents, and so occupying the last three feet of
       the line.

*Note:* the double cadence normally begins with a dactyl (for exceptions, see note 8), the triple cadence more often with a spondee. Vergil uses the triple cadence less than earlier poets, but it remains common with him too (see also under *Homodyne and Heterodyne* below).

*Rule 3   The First Part of the Line (before the Cadence)*

(a)   The first part of the line must contain at least one instance of alternation of ictus and accent before the caesura.  It need contain no coincidence at all before the cadence.

*Note:*   thus alternation can extend through consecutive spondees to a maximum of seven syllables (or nine, if an accented monosyllable or elided disyllable should precede the double cadence; see (b) below).

(b)   The cadence, double or triple, is normally preceded by an accent-free sequence beginning on or before the ictus immediately before it.

*Note:*   the effect of this rule is to create a 'low'-energy lull before the first stroke of the cadence, in which the pulse of the metre already emerges weakly, before then being reinforced by the coincidence of ictus and accent in the cadence.  If this ictus is immediately preceded by an accent, it forms part of an alternation, and the pulse of the metre only begins to emerge with the next unstressed syllable.

(c)   This rule is broken if, and only if, the cadence (double or triple) is immediately preceded by an accented mono-syllable, pyrrhic or elided disyllable.  The rule in fact presupposes that it is right *not* to accent these words in many or most cases.  As with Rule 1, so here, there will be a tendency for this rule, once accepted, to confirm itself, since it will make it seem natural not to accent monosyllables etc. just before the cadence unless there is a special reason for doing so.

*Note:*   the two rules (1 and 3(b)) taken together therefore tend towards regarding monosyllables etc. as unaccented unless there is a positive reason for stressing them, e.g. (*Aeneid* 2.2):

*inde toro pater Aeneas ⋮ sic orsus ab alto : //*
Then father Aeneas from his high couch thus started his story.

*Pater* is surely stressed here; the rules discourage accenting *sic* and that throws *orsus* into prominence.  (See also lines 7 and 22 of the analysis of the specimen text below).

(d)   The foot preceding the cadence typically contains an ictus but no accent, viz. the third foot before a triple cadence, the fourth foot before a double cadence (see further under *Homodyne and Heterodyne*, below).  A depart-ure from this norm requires the presence of a word of optional accent *and* a decision to accent it.

*Note:* the fourth foot, of course, often contains an accent *coinciding* with the ictus, so forming the beginning of a triple cadence. For coincidence in the third foot, see note at the end of the *Analysis of the Specimen Text*, below.


## Homodyne and Heterodyne

These terms have become fashionable to describe coincidence and alternation of ictus and accent respectively. They are usually applied to feet, sometimes to words. In particular, it is often stated that the last two feet of the hexameter are normally homodyne, while the first four are (in Vergil) predominantly heterodyne, and that Vergil's advance over his predecessors was to make the fourth foot predominantly hetero-dyne rather than homodyne, as it was before him.

One problem with this nomenclature is that some feet have no accent and others have two (so for instance in *Aeneid* 2.2 quoted above,the fourth foot has no accent, the first has two. More importantly, perhaps, the situation outlined in Rule 3(b)-(d) above means that the idea of a heterodyne fourth foot is wrong. Typically, the fourth foot is 'monodyne' (if that will serve to describe a foot with only one kind of stress); but in fact it is not the fourth foot as such, but the foot before the cadence, double or triple, which is 'monodyne'. The change that Vergil made is that he less frequently uses the triple cadence, thereby making the fourth foot less often homodyne, more often 'monodyne' - but still rather rarely heterodyne (unless of course monosyllables etc. are, after all, regularly accented).

It is, however, still useful to be able to say that the hexameter moves from a predominantly heterodyne first part to a uniformly homodyne ending, and that it is very rare to find a completely homodyne line such as *Aeneid* 4.486:

spárgens úmida mélla soporiferúmque papáuer
dropping oozy  honey and the sleepy poppy.


## Analysis of Ictus-accent Interplay in the Specimen Text

(*Note:* in addition to the terms 'coincidence' and 'alternation', we shall here use the term 'low' for a sequence containing an ictus but no accent, as defined in Rule 3(b) above.)

Line

1    With *postquam-, in-* and *atque-* unaccented, and *uentum-* accented, we have continuous alternation over seven syllables, a low fourth foot and double cadence, with five accents altogether:

*postquam-altos uentum-in montis : atque-inuia lustra , //*

2     One coincidence, one alternation of syllables, a low
     third foot and triple cadence, with six accents altogether:

*ecce ferae saxi : deiecrae uertice caprae /*

3     With *de* unaccented, there are two coincidences, one
     alternation of three syllables (containing a major pause,
     however); a low, beginning in the third foot, and double
     cadence, with six accents altogether:

*decurrere iugis; : // alia de parte patentis/*

4     With unaccented *atque-*, there is continuous alternation
     over seven syllables, a lo  fourth foot and double
     cadence, with five accents altogether:

*transmittunt cursu :/campos atque-agmina cerui /*

5     Two coincidences, an alternation of three syllables, a
     low, beginning in the third foot, and a double cadence,
     with six accents altogether:

*puluerulenta fuga : glomerant montisque relinquunt. //*

6     With *in* unaccented, we have to decide between:

*at puer, or at puer, or at puer,*

giving one coincidence or none, two or three alternations of
two syllables, a low, beginning in the third foot, and
a double cadence, with five or six accents altogether, e.g.:

*at puer Ascanius : mediis in uallibus acri /*

7     If *iamque-*, *hos* and *iam* were all accented, there would
     be eight accents altogether, and no low. Without allow-
     ing this to influence our decision, let us take the three
     words in context: it seems right either to accent both
     *iam*'s or neither; if both, we have either:
*iamque-hos cursu, iam praeterit illos*, or *iamque-hos*
*cursu, iam praeterit illos*, of which certainly the first
seems overloaded and unsuited to the sense; in the second
the effect of the strong repeated *iam*'s must now be
weighed against the third possibility:
*iamque-hos cursu, iam praeterit illos*, with the strong
balance of *hos ... illos* and the greater prominence gain-
ed for *praeterit*. In this version we would have one
coincidence, one alternation of two and one of three
(since in *hos cursu* the accent on *cur-* neutralises the
impression of coincidence on *hos*), a low fourth foot
and double cadence, with six accents altogether:

gaudet equo / iamque-hos : cursu, / iam praeterit illos, //

8    If *pecora-* can be treated as an unaccented pyrrhic, we
would have two coincidences, one alternation of two
syllables, a low third foot and triple cadence, with six
accents altogether:

spumantemque dari : pecora-inter inertia uotis /

      If *pecora-* is accented (Ascanius might well stress *pe-*
as he says *pecora inertia* to himself in impatient scorn,
though the effect would be surer if the sounds recurred
somewhere nearby), then we have two coincidences, one
alternation of three syllables, a truly heterodyne foot
before the triple cadence, and seven accents altogether:

spumantemque dari : pecora-inter inertia uotis /

9    With *aut* unaccented and *aprum-* accented, we have one
coincidence, an alternation of four syllables, a low
third foot and triple cadence, with six accents altogether:

optat aprum, aut fuluum : descendere monte leonem. //

10    One alternation of two and one of three, a low third
foot and triple cadence, with five accents altogether:

Interea magno : misceri murmure caelum /

11    One coincidence, an alternation of two syllables, a low,
beginning in the second foot, before a triple cadence,
and five accents altogether:

incipit, / insequitur : commixta grandine nimbus; //

12    With the opening *et* unaccented, the second *et* prodelided
and *passim* therefore accented, we have two alternations
of two and one of three, a low fourth foot and double
cadence, with five accents altogether:

et Tyrii comites : passim-et Troiana iuuentus /

13    Two coincidences, an alternation of three syllables, a
low fourth foot and double cadence, with six accents
altogether:

Dardaniusque nepos : Veneris diuersa per agros /

14    With *de* unaccented, we have two coincidences, two alternations of two syllables, a low fourth foot and double
cadence, with six accents altogether:

tecta metu petiere; // ruunt : de montibus amnes. //

15  With *et* unaccented and *dux* accented, we have continuous
    alternation over seven syllables, a low fourth foot and
    double cadence, with five accents altogether:

    speluncam Dido : dux et Troianus eandem  /

16  With the two *et*'s unaccented (the first probably being
    prodelided), we have one alternation of two and one
    of five syllables, a low fourth foot and double cadence,
    with five accents altogether:

    deueniunt. // prima— et Tellus: et pronube Iuno  /

17  With *et* and probably *dant* (unobtrusive before the
    important *signum*) unaccented, and the elided *fulsere-*
    accented as *fulser-*, we would have continuous alter-
    nation over seven syllables, a low fourth and double
    cadence, with five accents altogether:

    dant signum; // fulsere-:ignes, / et conscius Aether  /

    Accenting *fulsere-* would give two alternations of three
    syllables (see line 7 above for the 'neutralising' of a
    coincidence), and five accents altogether.  Judgment
    here depends on whether *fulsere* makes more impact by
    preserving the stress on its stem, or by the enhanced
    impact of *-sere* (bearing in mind the neutralising effect
    just mentioned) after the unstressed *ful-* *:

    dant signum; // fulsere-:ignes, / et conscius Aether  /

18  With elided *-que-* giving *summoque-*, we have one alter-
    nation of two and one of three syllables, a low third
    foot and triple cadence, with five accents altogether:

    conubiis / summoque-:ululararunt uertice nymphae. //

19  One coincidence, one alternation of six syllables, a low
    fourth foot and double cadence, with six accents alto-
    gether:

    ille dies primus : leti primusque malorum  /

20  With *neque-* unaccented, we have one coincidence, one alter-
    nation of two syllables and another of three, a low,
    beginning in the third foot, and a double cadence, with
    six accents altogether:

    causa fuit; // neque-enim : specie famaue mouetur, //

---

* Coincidence on third ictus with following caesura is only possible
  if it is either an accented monosyllable (like *hoc* in line 22), or
  a word in vowel-junction retaining its accent, like *fulsere-* here.

21 With *nec* unaccented (like *neque* above), and *iam* accented (as the key word signalling the change), we have continuous alternation over seven syllables, a low fourth
foot and double cadence, with five accents altogether:

*nec iám furtíuum : Dído meditátur amórem; //*

22 With *uocat* clearly accented, the question is whether to
accent *hoc* or not. In both versions the line begins with
two alternations of two syllables and ends with a triple
cadence: with *hoc* accented there is no low, but a coincidence in an unusual position (see footnote to line 17
above) and six accents ; with *hoc* unaccented, we have
a low, in the third foot, before the triple cadence (and
five accents). The decision depends on getting the
right balance of emphasis between .hoc and *nomine*: in
the English equivalent, would we stress the phrase 'with
this name' more on 'this' or on 'name' or on both equally?
The juxtaposition of *nomine* and *culpam* also seems important; all in all, it seems better to reserve the emphasis
for *nomine* than to anticipate it on *hoc:*

*coniúgium uócat, / hóc : praetéxit nómine cúlpam. //*

This final line, together with lines 7, 8 and 17, illus-
trates how literary judgment seems to confirm the operation of the rules put forward here.

APPENDIX II B:

## Ictus-accent Interplay in Horace's Lyrics

What of the interplay of ictus and accent in the *Odes*?
We have to proceed with caution. We know that educated
Romans learned at school to drum out the rhythm of the
hexameter and, no doubt, of the pentameter also. As
mature readers, they could thus rely on an internalised sense
of the metre's flexible pattern of stresses, alongside their
instinctive awareness of natural word-accent. This surely
was not the case with the lyric systems which, apart from
some tentative experiments by Catullus, were something
quite new to Latin verse, as Horace himself so proudly
proclaims. Readers must have found, at least to begin
with, that they had to drum out these metres, sacrificing
word-accent in the process, just as they had done with
hexameters at school. Could it even be that these patterns
were so difficult to handle in Latin, that this was such a
*tour-de-force*, that Horace himself had to suppress his own
sense of word-accent in order to achieve it - and is this
at least part of the reason why he had no successors, why
the *Odes* did not start another flourishing new genre of
Latin verse derived from Greek models, like the hexameter
or elegiacs? These are powerful considerations, and they
certainly justify us in stressing the metres of the *Odes*
according to ictus alone.

Yet there remains the question: when the patterns of these
metres did become familiar - and, since they have virtually
fixed patterns, this might happen quickly enough with some
readers - what then? Indeed, we have to go a step further.
For ultimately the reality of ictus-accent interplay in
this poetry depends on what was going on in Horace's own
mind; and there, at least, these metres were surely as
deeply naturalised as the hexameter itself. Is it credible
that he simply suppressed word-accent in his mind from first
to last, and was never conscious of an aesthetic impact
arising from its interaction with the ictus, nor ever used it
for artistic effect? Systematic study will be needed to
throw more light on these questions. In the meantime, we
may make the following observations:

1. *In the Sapphic line*, the three longs immediately before
the mid-line break regularly show the ictus-accent-ictus
pattern, giving a powerful swell further reinforced by the
break itself; and it seems likely that this effect was a
factor, perhaps even a decisive factor, in causing Horace
to make a *long* fourth syllable and a regular fifth syllable
break normal in his Sapphic, as it was not in the Greek.
The line regularly ends with a single or double cadence,
formed by coincidence of the last one or two ictuses and accents

generally preceded by a 'low', e.g. 1.22:

> Integer uitae : scelerisque purus
>
> non éget Mauris : iaculis neque-arcu

Daunias latis : alit aesculetis, however, has an opening
coincidence and no 'low'.

2.   *The little Adonic line* regularly closes the Sapphic
stanza with double, i.e. total, coincidence (it is just
like a hexameter cadence), e.g.

> Fusce, pharetra, and arida nutrix (1.22).

3.   *The choriamb* ($\stackrel{\text{—}}{\cup}\cup\stackrel{\text{—}}{}$), which is the basic rhythm of the
Asclepiad systems, allows of *either* double coincidence,
or alternation at either end; e.g.:

> innumerabilis and imber edax (3.30); cui liquidam (1.24).

This last effect is ensured when a single word fills a
choriamb, e.g.:

> Melpómene (1.24)

Cf. the Greater Asclepiad line describing the winter seas
pounding the cliffs (1.11.5):

> quae nunc oppositis : debilitat : pumicibus mare

4.   *In the Lesser Asclepiad line*, there is a tendency for
alternation to predominate in the first half and coincidence
in the second, but with the final ictus ensuring a sense of
alternation to close, being *either* continuous over the last
three syllables, e.g.:

> Ouis multa gracilis : te puer in rosa (1.5.1),

or across three syllables with an unstressed in the middle:

> perfusus liquidis : urget odoribus (1.5.2)

- cf. the end of the pentameter. Note that the ictus-accent-
ictus pattern over three longs, as seen in both the above
examples, is common in this line, but not characteristic of
it, as it is in the middle of the Sapphic line (see 1 above).

5.   *The Glyconic line* ranges from total coincidence (but for
the effect of the final ictus as noted under 4 above) to
total alternation, e.g.:

> puro numine Iuppiter and Tyrrhenus genuit parens. (3.10)

6.   *The Pherecratean line* regularly shows total coincidence
over its first six syllables, which is then dislocated by the
final ictus on the seventh, giving alternation at the end, e.g.:

grãto, Pýrrha, sub ãntro? (1.5)

This effect is crucial; without it, the line becomes like a
hexameter triple cadence, sometimes leading on into a
Glyconic with total coincidence in a way which would
produce a monotonous homodyne sequence over six
ictuses, e.g. later in the same *Ode*:

nígris aéquora uéntis /

émirãbitur ínsolens,

The alternation and the minor pause at the end of the
Pherecratean make all the difference, and vindicate the
scansion of the line with two consecutive ictuses at the
end, cf. Catullus' Limping Iambic below.  Moreover, the
fact that the first six syllables of this line regularly have
a homodyne pattern whereas the same sequence is rather
variable in the Lesser Asclepiad and Glyconic, suggests
that Horace was sensitive to some particular effect here -
probably the skip-like effect at the end of the line, which
is only experienced if it is preceded by, and disrupts,
a smooth run.

7.    *The Alcaic hendecasyllable* (first and second lines of
the stanza) has the same second half as the Lesser Asclepiad
line, with its built-in effect of alternation at the end
(see 4 above).  Some lines would have total coincidence
but for this effect, e.g.:

pulsãnda téllus, : núnc Saliãribus (1.37)

Any of these coincidences may be replaced by an alternation,
but this is rare on the ictus immediately before the mid-line
break; this ensures that the first half ends with a light
or single cadence but not so the second half, so reversing
the relation between the two halves found in the Sapphic
hendecasyllable (see 1 above).  This subtle difference is
actually important, being required as part of the 'rising'
build-up of the Alcaic stanza into its third line, in contrast to the thrice-repeated rise-and-fall of the Sapphic.

8.    *In the third line of the Alcaic stanza*, total coincidence is possible, and there is always a light cadence, e.g.:

si frãctus íllabãtur órbis, (3.3)

But it is characteristic for alternation to predominate in the
middle of the line, where the build-up of the stanza reaches
its height.  An accent on the long fifth syllable (which Horace
required there, unlike his Greek model) produces this effect,
and Horace does seem fond of putting a word of three longs
into this position, and filling the line with three trisyllables
(or equivalents), e.g.:

ornãre púluinãr deórum and redégit in uéros timóres (1.37).

9.    *The fourth line of the Alcaic stanza* is a strongly
'falling' line, in which alternation tends to predominate
over the first two ictuses, but which regularly ends with
a single or double cadence, usually preceded by a 'low';
e.g.:

témpus érat dápibus, sodáles. clásses cíta repárauit óras;

and nón húmilis múlier triúmpho. (1.37).

*In conclusion*, the evidence here reviewed does suggest that
Horace was, at least to some extent, responding to, and making use of, the interaction of ictus and accent in his lyrics:
how far this went requires further study.  Some of the effects
may simply be consequences entailed in the syllabic pattern
of the metres; on the other hand, where that pattern contains
deliberate modifications of the Greek original by Horace (see
under 1 and 8 above), it seems particularly probable that
Latin word-accent was influencing him, as it certainly was
Ennius and the later Romans who adapted Homer's metre to
Latin (e.g. in virtually abolishing the 'weak' caesura).

APPENDIX IIC: Ictus-accent Interplay in Catullus


Here too there is a need for more systematic study of
Catullus' polymeters (indeed, of his elegiacs as well). We
may make the following observations:

The Phalaecian Hendecasyllable has an ending like that of the
Sapphic line (which is also a hendecasyllable), with a single
or double cadence, often preceded by a 'low'; but coincidence
readily extends back through the line, and total coincidence
is by no means unusual, e.g.:

      *omnes unius aestimemus assis* (5.3)

Alternation seems to be sought, however. This is rare at the
end, as in

      *nobis cum semel occidit breuis lux* (5.5),

but frequent in the familiar ictus-accent-ictus opening, e.g.:

      *Viuamus, mea Lesbia— atque-amemus* (5.1).

The homodyne tendency reinforces the absence of consecutive
longs and of a required break in mid-line to give the metre
its free, swinging movement - attractive as long as it does
not become monotonous or trivial, as it somehow might in
Latin without the energy-holding effect of some alternation.

A quite different, and unusual, effect is secured by the special
kind of alternation which results from two ictuses following
one another at the end of the 'limping', or perhaps 'skipping',
iambic. The rhythm -. inversion at the line-end also normally
ensures coincidence on the penultimate syllable, with a
strong stress in an unexpected position; from here alternation can extend back into the line e.g.:

      *Miser Catulle, : desinas ineptire* (8.1).

But it can also be the only variation in an otherwise homodyne line, e.g.:

      *at tu, Catulle, : destinatus obdura* (8.19).

In conclusion, it may be worth recalling that Catullus'
shorter poems did not undergo the careful, painstaking processes of composition - Horace's *labor limae*, 'the labour
of the file' - which underlie the text of Vergil's hexameters and Horace's lyrics. Whatever closer scrutiny might
reveal, we should remember that in these Catullan metres
a poet's ear is working in a still relatively untried and
unfamiliar medium.

APPENDIX III:

The Pronunciation of Vowel-Junctions (Elisions)


As we saw in Part IV, Latin speakers evidently experienced
a *hiatus* or 'gap' in passing from one vowel to another between two words, and the rules of Latin metre are clearly designed to eliminate this phenomenon, except at the line-end
or as an exception within the line, by requiring the elision
or 'knocking out' of the first vowel at every such vowel-
junction. Naturally enough, this has also been the traditional practice in reading Latin verse, consistent with an
entirely metrical stressing of the words (see Part VI). And,
before going any further, it is only fair to quote W.S. Allen
(*Vox Latina*, p.93):

> However, if the English reader chooses to apply
> elision in all cases of vowel-junction, and
> thereby avoid the uncertainties inherent in
> other solutions, he will at any rate be no
> further removed from Classical practice than
> the Latin grammarians were; and only rarely
> will such reading lead to real ambiguity.

Yet, as Allen also shows, there is good reason for thinking
that uniform elision was not the normal practice in Classical
times. Even some Anglo-Saxon writers, finding uniform elision unsatisfactory, have taken to using a different term
(long familiar on the continent) for what happens at vowel-
junctions, i.e. *synaloepha*, a Greek word meaning a 'running
or blending together'. What makes the whole subject particularly tantalising is that, by general agreement, this
phenomenon (whether called elision of synaloepha) is supposed to produce all kinds of subtle artistic effects at
many vowel-junctions in Latin verse - unlike Greek, where
such effects are hardly seen as figuring at all. Yet we
have to insist that, to be *real*, these effects must arise
out of what is actually *said and heard* at these vowel-
junctions.

It is worth noting the objections which our ears register
against uniform elision, once we are hearing Latin poetry
spoken, rather than seeing it on the page. Firstly, it sometimes creates just the kind of hiatus which it is supposed
to eliminate, e.g. *Aeneid* 1.30: *Troas, reliquias Dana(um)-
atque*. Secondly, it does regularly produce slight ambigui-
ties, for instance between the singular and plural of neuter
nouns and adjectives of the 2nd declension, e.g. *Aeneid*
1.281: *consili—in melius referet*. Did Vergil write
*consilium* or *consilia*?

It is true that serious ambiguity is rare. But the frequent

loss of inflectional endings makes it harder for the ear
to follow the sense.  Take these lines in which Aeneas
awakes and climbs on to the roof of his home in Troy.
With uniform elision, this is what we hear (*Aeneid*
2.302-3):

> *excutior somn-et summi fastigia tecti*
> *ascensu super atqu-arrectis auribus asto.*

*Somn* must be *somno* (not *somni* or *somnum*); *super* cannot
be the word *super*, but must be *supero*.  This is confusing
even to a native speaker, and seems intrinsically improb-
able.  On the other hand, the elision of *atque* feels per-
fectly natural.

Thirdly, and independently of any problems of comprehension,
the loss of a final *long* vowel, including diphthongs and
nasalised final vowels in -*m*, often give a Latin word a
sense of disfigurement.

And so, many readers nowadays go to the opposite extreme,
pronouncing in full both vowels at every vowel-junction.
They thereby turn every vowel-junction into a hiatus,
and introduce an extra syllable for which there is no room
in the metre - and this can happen three times in one line,
as in line 1 of the specimen text.  Such a style of reading vowel-junctions is consistent with the 'as prose'
stressing mentioned in Part VII, even though hiatus was
seemingly also largely avoided in prose and ordinary speech.
In verse, with no recognition of ictus, and with extra
syllables at vowel-junctions, there is nothing left of
the metre except the cadence; but, to our ears at least,
regular hiatus seems preferable to the constant mutilation
of words and grammatical imprecision of uniform elision.

In the face of this dilemma, it does seem worthwhile embarking on the 'uncertainties inherent in other solutions'
(Allen, op.cit.), to see if we can construct some guidelines which are both acceptable in theory and serviceable
in practice.  Now it seems very likely that, in this matter
of vowel-junctions as in some others (such as, for instance,
the accenting of monosyllables), the actual practice of
speakers in Vergil's own time was complex and variable, and
that even if we had recordings to listen to, no simple or
uniform procedure would emerge.  It is therefore quite
reasonable for each of us to construct our own reading of
vowel-junctions out of the various options that offer themselves.  These seem to be five in number:  elision of the
first vowel, elision of the second vowel, contraction of
the two vowels, changing the final vowel into a consonantal
*y* or *w*, and retention of both vowels.

*Elision of the First Vowel (Post-elision)*

A distinction is sometimes drawn between 'heavy' and 'light' elision. The latter involves the loss of a final *short* vowel, the former of a final *long* vowel, including diphthongs and the nasalised vowels in -*m*. A very rough guide based on this distinction would be to avoid heavy elision, and use light elision in the following cases:

1. A few words ending in short -*i*: *mihi, tibi, sibi, ibi* and *ubi*.

2. Words ending in short -*a*, i.e. 1st declension feminine singulars and 2nd declension neuter plurals.

3. A large range of words ening in short -*e*, including active infinitives, 3rd person perfect plurals in -*ere*, some imperatives, 3rd declension ablative singulars and neuter nominative and accusative singulars, etc.; perhaps also, incidentally, a few words ending in long -*e*, especially the pronouns *me, te, se, sese*.

In practice, we may often prefer one of the other options even to light elision, especially of the case-ending in -*a*. There is, however, one clear recommendation: final -*que* (also -*ue* and -*ne*) should always be elided, and the accent adjusted to be that of the remaining whole word, e.g. *súmmo*, which becomes *summóque*, but reverts to *súmmoqu* at a vowel-junction like *súmmóque-ululárunt* (specimen text, line 18).

*Elision of the second vowel (Prodelision)*

Sometimes we see a combination such as *bonum est* actually printed in our texts as *bonumst*. It is the initial vowel of the second word that has been elided. This procedure may suit the following cases: *est* (but not when accented, e.g. when meaning 'there is'); *et, ac* and *atque; ex* and *in* (perhaps also *ab* and *ad*), whether as prepositions or at the beginning of longer words, always provided they are not accented. Examples of the above include: *Teucrorum-(e)x oculis* (*Aeneid* 1.89); *postquam-(e)xempta fames* (*Aeneid* 1. 216); and *ac ueluti magno-(i)n populo cum saepe coorta-(e)st* (*Aeneid* 1.148).

There is one common situation in which the prodelision of *et, ac* and *atque* is particularly attractive. Take a line like *Aeneid* 1.151: *tum, pietate grauem-ac meritis si forte uirum quem.* Here the word for 'and' stands, according to the metre, just *before* the caesura, whereas in sense it belongs closely with the next word. By using prodelision in such a case we get a more natural reading: *tum pietate grauem-'c metitis.*

In the case of *atque*, pronounced *acque*, we often find that
it stands *between* two vowel junctions, and is quite naturally elided at both ends, leaving what we actually say and
hear as *'cqu'*. Here again are the lines about Aeneas climb-
ing on to the roof as they might actually sound (*Aeneid* 2.
302-3):

*excutior somno:'t summi fastigia tecti*
*ascensu supero:'cqu' arrectis auribus asto.*

So frequent is the word 'and' that, by eliding -*que* and
by prodeliding *et* and *atque*, we shall find that we have
disposed at one stroke of a considerable proportion of
the vowel-junctions in Vergil's text, or more precisely
of what we might call the 'light' vowel-junctions, where
literary effects would not generally be expected.

*Contraction of the Two Vowels into One Vowel or Diphthong*

This is the 'drawing together' of two vowels belonging to
different words into one vowel or diphthong, so as to run
or blend together (true *synaloepha*). This sometimes happens
between syllables *within* a word e.g. *Aeneid* 2.131: *dehinc ita*
*fatur* =*deinc ita fatur*. At a vowel-junction between two words,
either the vowels may be the same and are simply pronounced
only once, e.g. *Aeneid* 2.132: *iamque dies infanda-aderat;*
or a long may absorb a short, e.g.*Aeneid* 2.102 : *uno-ordine.*

Where the two vowels are different, they may create a
diphthong, whose spelling may look odd on the page, but
which is in fact readily assimilated to one of the standard
diphthongs of Latin: *ae, au, ei, eu* or *oe*. Some examples
are: *ae: consilia-in melius referet* (*Aeneid* 1.281); *au:*
*maria-omnia circum* (*Aeneid* 1.32); *ei: saepe-illos* (*Aeneid*
2.110); *eu: adsensere-omnes* (*Aeneid* 2.130); *oe: infando-*
*indicio* (*Aeneid* 2.84).

What of the nasalised long vowels represented by vowel +
*m*? There seems no reason why final -*am*, -*em* and -*om* should
not in some cases contract with the following vowel (for
-*im* and -*um* see under next section). This would form a
nasalised long vowel or diphthong (marked with the cedilla
underneath) which can be pronounced as its plain, unnasalised
equivalent if preferred. Some examples are: the same vowel:
*patriam antiquam* = *patriantiquam* (*Aeneid* 2.137), which could
also be thought of as a prodelision; *ae: nequiquam-ingrata* =
*nequiquaingrata* (*Aeneid* 2.101); *au: quemquam-aut* = *quemquaut*
(*Aeneid* 2.127); *ei: insontem-infando-indicio* = *insonteinfando-*
*indicio* (*Aeneid* 2.84); *eu: scitantem-oracula* = *scitanteoracula*
(*Aeneid* 2.114). It is worth noting that, in some of these
instances, one reader might prefer prodelision, another
contraction, e.g. *nequiquam'ngrata* or *nequiquaingrata*.

*Changing the final vowel into a Consonantal y or w (Synizesis)*

This Greek word meaning 'setting or sitting together' describes
two vowels sharing a place normally reserved for just one: it
ought to refer to the kind of contraction we have just been
looking at. In fact the word is mainly used in cases where
the first vowel is *i* or *u*; and what happens there is not
that it shares a place with the next vowel, but that it turns
into a *y* or *w*. This can happen *inside* a word, e.g. *intexunt
abiete costas* (Aeneid 2.16), which has to be read as *intexunt
abyete costas*. Similarly, at a vowel-junction we can have:
*se signari-oculis = se signaryoculis* (Aeneid 12.3); and
*hunc tu olim = hunc twolim* (Aeneid 1.289).

Next, we can extend the procedure to final -e and -o, perhaps
also -ae; again, we find it happening *within* a word, as in
*antehac = antyac*. So we could also have: *fatale-adgressi*
(pronounced *aggressi*) = *fatalyaggressi* (Aeneid 2.165);
*fando-aliquod = fandwaliquod* (Aeneid 2.81); *arae-ensesque =
aryensesque* (Aeneid 2.155).

Can we go still further, and extend the procedure to nasal
vowels? It could mean changing them into nasal semivowels,
y and w. Now, so far as we know, Latin did not elsewhere
use these sounds. But they do occur, and precisely at
vowel-junctions, in Vedic Sanskrit. Dare we suppose that
this also happened in Latin, and so pronounce final -*em*
and -*im* as y, final -*om* and -*um* as w? It is above all the
multitude of final -*um*'s that makes this possibility so
attractive. Some possible examples are: *huc septem-Aeneas
= huc septyAeneas* (Aeneid 1.170); *insontem-infando =
insontyinfando* (Aeneid 2.84), as an alternative to contraction; *imperium-Oceano = imperiyOceano* (Aeneid 1.287);
*uenturum-excidio Libyae = uenturwexcidio Libyae* (Aeneid
1.22), where prodelision is also possible. If we shrink
from this procedure, not so much out of tenderness of
philological conscience, but because these nasal noises
seem hard to make, we can simply use plain y and w to
represent final -*em* and -*um*.

One final point, on which Indo-European philology again
offers help. Sometimes the result of turning a final vowel
into a y or w (plain or nasal) would be to make the
preceding syllable long where the metre requires it to
be short. The solution is to treat such cases in the same
way as Latin sometimes treats r as a second consonant which
allows the preceding syllable to be either long or short
e.g. *pātria* or *pătria*; *tenēbrae* or *tenĕbrae*. So at
Aeneid 1.260 we would have: *magnanimum-Aenean = magnănĭmwAenean*.

*Retention of Both Vowels*

Occasionally, a special need to pause at a vowel-junction may
make it most natural to pronounce both vowels in full, with
a pause between, hiatus and extra syllable notwithstanding,
e.g. *Aeneid* 2.241:

*O patria, // O diuum domus Ilium-et incluta bello /,*

where keeping the final *-a* in *patria* suggests a break in
the speaker's voice, but where the vowel-junction *Ilium-
et* should be rendered either by prodelision as *Ilium't*,
with some lingering on the *-um*, or, by using a semi-vowel,
as *Iliwet*, where any lingering would come on the long *I*
of *Ilium*. Cf. *Aeneid* 2.172:

*uix positum castris simulacrum: // arsere coruscae*

where the choice is between retention and a marked pause,
or a semi-vowel = *simulacrᵧarsere*, with some lingering
on *-acr-*.

*Personal Style and Poetic Artistry*

In the pronunciation of vowel-junctions, there can be no
'right' or 'wrong'. We can adopt a uniform procedure,
by always eliding or by never eliding, and accept the
drawbacks for the sake of simplicity. If we do venture
into the subtleties of other options, then we find that
often there is more than one way of pronouncing a particular
vowel-junction. Always we should be guided in our choice by
our ear and our judgment - our feeling for the sound and
for the sense. We should not aim at being consistent in
practice, always pronouncing the same combination of vowels
in the same way. Rather, we should respond in each case
to the words in which those vowels stand, and to their
context, and read in the way that sounds right to us at
the time.

It is generally agreed that Vergil chose not to smoothe
away all vowel-junctions out of his text (as Ovid liked to do
and Horace in his *Odes*), because he wanted this coarse
grain in the texture of his verse; and many are the literary
effects attributed to these vowel-junctions. With uniform
elision, all this must be supposed to arise from the
mutilation of words (especially as these effects and this
coarse grain are particularly seen in *heavy* elision). With
uniform retention, all this would presumably be supposed to
arise from hiatus and the dislocation of the metre. It does
seem that a combination of the various resources we have
been reviewing offers a more likely medium for verbal artistry to a poetic craftsman like Vergil. To test this out,
here is a listing of the vowel-junctions from *Aeneid* 4.
450-73, in which Dido forms her decision to take her own life: